MW01114534

Unfinished conversations:
On democracy, race, the economy, and a path forward

By Konstanze Frischen and Michael Zakaras

Published by
Unfinished LLC
888 Seventh Ave, 16th Floor
New York, NY 10106

UNFINISHED
www.unfinished.com

Design by Felicidad Pública
Illustrations by Lennard Kok

ISBN: 978-0-578-25301-5

Unfinished conversations:
On democracy, race, the economy, and a path forward

Contents

Foreword

I grew up in a household of seven siblings. Almost every evening at dinner-time, we would gather around the table with my parents—and, often, other family members and friends—and discuss current events. With so many people and so many opinions, those dinners made for lively, interesting conversations. We learned to listen. We argued. But every time I or my siblings complained about a policy or an action or an incident, my parents would ask: "What are you going to do about it?"

That question has stayed with me throughout my life and shaped my identity as a builder, as a business leader, and as a civic entrepreneur. I'm interested in examining the root cause of an issue and then finding ways to implement solutions and make transformational change. Often, that means looking for new approaches and defying common wisdom. It requires starting at the source and stripping away the noise and the gridlock that frequently prevent progress. Ultimately, it's about showing up in the world in a responsible way—holding yourself and others accountable through active, integrated, persistent work that results in positive change and creates a legacy that can be built upon by future generations.

We are living at a time of incredible opportunity. The world has more abundant resources than ever before. Technology has given us access to new ideas and new markets. We have the ability to connect with one another in ways that were impossible just a few decades ago. Changes in the way that we live, work, and interact are opening the doors to once-unimaginable progress.

And yet, even in the midst of this moment of promise, we are too often unable to find common ground. In our economy, the playing field is divided between the lucky and the left out. In our democracy, powerful individuals and industries are making it more difficult for everyday people to be heard and creating obstacles to necessary change. In our technology ecosystems, monopolistic companies are setting the terms of the conversation—cutting off competition, centralizing control, and harming civic dialogue.

We are becoming more polarized and more disconnected and are collectively losing confidence in our institutions when collaboration is more important than ever. We are losing one of the most important pillars of our common life: trust. On issues from climate change to economic development to racism to gun violence, today's polarization makes it impossible to make meaningful strides forward—and our approach to problem-solving too often involves imposing solutions without input from impacted populations. When we do speak to the people who are affected, it is frequently to confirm our own viewpoints or justify our assumptions.

But what if we approached problems differently? What if we listened to people who are close to the issues, close to the pain, and close to the impact of our proposed solutions without judgment or preconceptions? What if we began real conversations designed to help us more fully understand one another?

The conversations that follow are intended to achieve exactly that: to provide us with insights that come directly from people who are close to the issues at hand, and are from communities that are underrepresented in our national dialogue. The interviews take place with a collection of Ashoka Fellows—social entrepreneurs who are working to champion new ideas and transform our society for the better.

I was introduced to Ashoka several years ago and immediately was drawn to its core mission: to find the people with the big ideas and surround them with what they need to be successful. That includes a peer network where Ashoka Fellows can regularly learn from one another, open doors for each other, and spot patterns within and across fields. When you meet a Fellow— or for that matter, some of the exceptional people who work at Ashoka (and who conducted the interviews that follow)—you can't help but be more optimistic about the future. They are out there, working on the very things that keep us up at night. They show us what is possible. And they inspire us.

The individuals interviewed in the following pages represent a range of backgrounds and work in a variety of fields, but what they share is a perspective on some of our most urgent challenges based on lived experiences, and an approach to problem-solving that puts communities at the center. Their expertise is in untangling real problems for real people—and their perspectives are not heard nearly enough.

Together, they speak about issues that are small and large, and share innovative ideas that open up new pathways for advancement. How to revitalize Appalachia by investing in organic growth and human potential, and allow the region to lead clean energy development. How to support fishing communities through regenerative ocean farming to narrow inequality, improve sustainability, and create bonds between white working-class fishermen and Indigenous people. How to end poverty, improve democracy, save lives, unleash potential, and revive human dignity in ways that are ambitious, exciting, and transformational.

Effectively addressing these challenges won't come from top-down interventions or be imposed unilaterally by well-meaning individuals or organizations. Instead, they will come from collective action—from a process that lifts up the people who are most impacted and least heard. This grassroots approach is what's required to break us out of our bubbles and join us together in a shared, often messy, and sometimes contradictory effort to design our common future.

At a time when it can be difficult to communicate with one another over the noise of partisan gridlock, these impact leaders are speaking candidly about what politicians and advocates on both sides of the aisle often get wrong about their communities. They are sharing how a different approach can result in effective progress. And they are demonstrating how overlooked ideas can help get us unstuck. That is, at the most fundamental level, why I launched Unfinished: to rebuild trust and drive progress and inclusion by elevating new voices and forging unexpected alliances.

The perspectives in the pages that follow are not often at the forefront of our collective national dialogue. They are rarely quoted in the news or shared in boardrooms across the country. They don't fit easily into the boxes we too often create for ourselves and others. But they are shaped by real-life experiences, informed by conversations with impacted communities, and attuned to the kind of impact we can make if we listen to one another and take action together. They might not be front-page or breaking news, but I like to think they represent a better picture of who we really are.

Of course, the challenges we face in communities across the country are wide-ranging and multifaceted, and no single solution will move us where we need to go. These interviews are not intended to provide simple answers to difficult problems. Instead, this collection is intended to urge us to listen and then start meaningful conversations—the kind that I was so fortunate to have at my family's dinner table—about the way that we approach challenges and the steps we can take to move forward together.

So: What are you going to do about it?

Frank McCourt
Chairman and CEO, Unfinished

About This Book

What does the United States look like from the standpoint of the people working to make it better? That is the central guiding question behind this book. It is a book of windows: windows into the minds of some of the most creative social entrepreneurs and movement builders you'll ever encounter. Windows into the cities and towns and people from across the nation they work with—fishermen and coal miners, gun owners and small-town mayors, Black environmentalists, teachers, small-business owners, Navajo women, high school students and their parents and neighbors. Windows into the dynamism of our country.

Changemakers are everywhere. But when they live outside established circles, their perspectives are rarely sought, or at best seen as tangential to policy discussions. Their stories remain unheard or underappreciated. How can that be? We are living through a period of tremendous upheaval: a devastating global pandemic, an accelerating climate crisis, a racial reckoning, a hobbled democracy, and rising inequities of all kinds. These are public problems. They can feel unrelenting. Yet while we hunger for solutions, we too often turn to the same people and same voices, somehow expecting different outcomes.

In these chapters, we listen to innovators *for the public*. Twenty of them, in fact. At first glance, they are extremely different. They grew up on the coast of Newfoundland and in West Virginia and in Oklahoma. They live in Atlanta and San Jose and in the Mississippi Delta. They are former journalists, former assembly-line workers, former White House staff, former teachers. They come from conservative families, religious families, civil rights activist families. They work in courthouses and on farms, with Black Lives Matter and with police officers, with billionaire philanthropists and former presidents, with people who are incarcerated and with undocumented teenagers. They are White and Black and Brown and Indigenous.

But these changemakers are also similar in important ways. First, they all live in close proximity to the social problems they are trying to solve. Many have experienced those problems personally. It's one reason why they are so profoundly empathetic, and they use that empathy to shape their ideas, policies, and movements. Their intimate, practical knowledge means what they are doing is more likely to work and more likely to last. It is the difference between cleverness—which is abundant in the world of tech start-ups and social enterprises—and wisdom, which is in short supply.

Their vantage points deepen our understanding of each other. The writer and artist Chimamanda Ngozi Adichie warns about the danger of what she calls the "single story"—a story that, while true, is incomplete and therefore reinforces stereotypes. Adichie is from Nigeria and went to college in the United States. Her first roommate there, probably like most Americans still, knew a single story of Africa: a continent of beautiful animals and of people dying of poverty and AIDS. The problem with the "single story" is it quickly becomes the only story. It strips down a person or a place to one often unflattering dimension and makes it harder to see our shared humanity. We are awash in these simplified stories today: of the heartland or the coastal elites or the blue-collar workers or the winners versus the losers.

These changemakers do the opposite: They *add* dimensions. They invite us to question our stereotypes and define others by their assets and aspirations, rather than their weaknesses and deficits (chapter 5, Trabian Shorters). They remind us that only a few of us are natives and most of us are descendants of immigrants (chapter 11, Laura Emiko Soltis). They point out that poor people are deeply resourceful and strategic (chapter 6, Mauricio Lim Miller), and that we all need a sense of belonging and meaningful relationships to thrive (chapter 14, Sarah Hemminger). What they are saying, quite simply—to philanthropists, to policy makers, to anyone serious about advancing positive social change—is this: Start by listening.

Second, the protagonists of this book are what we call "systems changers." That's jargon for what is a pretty straightforward idea: They are driven to address root causes rather than treat symptoms. It's the difference between pulling plastic waste out of your local river day after day and going to the source of where it enters the river in the first place. It is the difference between building more homeless shelters in your city and eliminating the main causes of chronic homelessness (chapter 19, Rosanne Haggerty). Systems changers will ask: What are the underlying factors that still make it harder for Black Americans to access capital and start businesses (chapter 17, Tim Lampkin)? They dismantle the conditions that allow inequities to persist in the first place because they have witnessed what does not work and they are tired of seeing Band-Aids applied to deep societal failures.

Third, there's an underlying insight beneath the critiques and solutions offered in this book: Successful social change works when the changemaking energy of those closest to the problem gets unleashed. When community members participate, have agency, and a say. When people from all walks of life play a role in shaping a better way forward. While in this book we highlight individual leaders, they will be the first to tell you that their real power comes from the people and communities they partner with.

It's an important distinction, the difference between solving problems *for* others and solving them *with* others—in fact, letting "others" lead. This is the hidden magic of social entrepreneurs: demonstrating time and time again not just how to merge entrepreneurial creativity with social change, but how to recruit citizens across the world to step in and shape their communities for the better.

What does this look like in practice? It comes in the form of family members and neighbors participating in the legal defense of a loved one accused of a crime to change case outcomes and reduce thousands of years of cumulative prison time (chapter 9, Raj Jayadev). It shows up in the fishermen who are reinventing themselves as restorative ocean farmers who feed us while slowing climate change (chapter 1, Bren Smith). And in the millions of Black women walking in neighborhoods across America to reclaim their health and fight for a better world for their daughters and granddaughters (chapter 2, T. Morgan Dixon). You see it in the application of Indigenous wisdom passed down through generations to address modern health challenges (chapter 8, Denisa Livingston). And in the way young people living in the child welfare system are leading efforts to improve that system (chapter 13, Sixto Cancel).

When that happens—when everyone becomes a changemaker—people come together and the barriers that divide us begin to dissolve. The commitment is to the problem in front of them. And as people work on solving it in pluralist teams, they build shared experience and empathy with those they might otherwise assume they have little in common with. That includes listening to those who are fearful of new immigrants and inviting them into conversation with refugees to explore how to make their towns more welcoming (chapter 3, David Lubell). It means cutting past red/blue divides and working to boost civic participation and spirit at the local level as partisans for *democracy* (chapter 20, Eric Liu). It means recognizing our common interest in reducing gun violence and gun suicides, and bringing together gun owners and those vehemently opposed to guns to collaborate (chapter 4, Casey Woods). These approaches help us spot, and then build from, a place of agreement, and a spirit of mutuality.

The last thing the group of twenty innovators we spoke to for this book have in common is that they are all Ashoka Fellows—selected into our organization's global network precisely because of these shared attributes and because of their commitment to equity and the common good. When they become Fellows, they benefit from participation in a lifelong peer learning community that spans every continent of the globe, and that is designed to help their ideas go farther faster.

The curators and editors of this book work at Ashoka, the world's largest network of social entrepreneurs. One of us is a recent immigrant; one has lived in the U.S. most of his life. We both talk about how lucky we feel to see this country through the lens of what is possible—and what is working. We put this book together because we believe the insights and voices portrayed in these pages are what we should learn from and turn to in a world of unprecedented change and upheaval. Many of the answers are out there. And they are working. American renewal is happening all around us, behind the decentralized leadership and wisdom of changemakers like those we spoke to in this book. Their road map starts to emerge in the pages that follow. It's up to us to follow their lead.

One more thing to note: This is a book of conversations. Each chapter is an interview, lightly edited for length and clarity. We could have asked our contributors to write short essays or op-eds, but we preferred the informality and the spontaneity of an interview. No prepared questions, no talking points. Just honest reflection about what they are seeing and where we need to go.

We would like to thank our partners at Unfinished, including Frank McCourt and Paula Recart, who invited and supported Ashoka to write this book. Thank you also to our many Ashoka colleagues for enabling this work, and of course to the twenty featured Ashoka Fellows for their insights and honesty. We are deeply appreciative for the role they play in moving us all toward a better future.

Konstanze Frischen and Michael Zakaras
Ashoka

Jobs You Write Songs About

Bren Smith

Bren Smith is a fisherman turned ocean farmer. On vertical farms below the sea surface, ocean farmers grow kelp, oysters, and scallops—with zero fertilizer, freshwater or feed—in a way that sequesters nitrogen and carbon out of the ocean. The winning argument for ocean farming is not the appeal to save the planet. It's the appeal to save oneself, to lead a self-determined life, to earn a living. A conversation about the need to reconcile ecology and economics, and overcome the class divide.

Bren, you care about the environment. A lot. And we want to talk with you about what the environmental movement got wrong.

Sure! I actually felt pretty alienated from the environmental movement for a long time. At one gathering I was invited to in the early times, to give a talk about transitions, they put up a picture of a coal worker with a dirty face, and it was meant to be like, "Oh, that poor coal worker, we are concerned about his health, the dirty coal," and so on. To me, the picture just looked like someone who's had a good day at work. There was a cultural difference that didn't sync well.

What is important in this context to know about the culture of your community?

I was forged in my youth by fishermen. Out of this hunter-gatherer tradition, the beauty and bounty of the high seas shaped my dreams and desires. The ocean gave me a job that I can sing a song about. It means being out at sea, alone, in a boat; it's about freedom, but it's also absolutely humbling. There's an incredible pride in feeding my country and community. But then, due to overfishing, the cod stocks collapsed in Newfoundland. Overnight, almost thirty thousand jobs disappeared. The fishing economy that got built up for literally hundreds of years got wiped out all of a sudden. And you realize: There will be no jobs on a dead ocean.

So with that background, that catastrophe going on, one would assume it would have been easy for you to find a place in the environmental movement. Why was that not the case?

Because they were framing it as "This is about birds, and bees, and bears" and not "This is about jobs and dignity." And the smart scientists were saying climate change is a hundred-year problem. And they were wrong, totally. Irene and Sandy had just come along and destroyed my farm. It turned out to be a here-and-now problem, not a slow lobster boil.

It wasn't until a group of fishermen and I hopped on my boat and went to the climate march in New York in 2014 that I felt like there's a place for me in the movement against climate change. At that march, I met farmers in Detroit building urban gardens. I met folks from Kentucky trying to solarize hollers. We talked. We all came from these working communities, from a sort of blue-collar innovation space where we've always been around people that are inventing stuff, scraping together. When you're poor, when you're working-class, you're having to invent every day to find a way to make it through this complex society. Because you don't have the resources. When you have resources, there's no necessity to be creative, right? And so I just met all these incredibly creative folks on that climate march who were hell-bent on building a movement around climate solutions. It felt for the first time like, "I found my home."

What would...

Hold on, there's more I want to say. Another problem. At that point, the environmental movement was functioning around the politics of no. Up until the emergence of the new politics of climate change in particular, you would always hear: "No to overfishing." "No to new pipelines." "Let's close down those coal plants." "Don't eat this or that." "Let's stop urban sprawl." It's the politics of no. And of course, I get it, we need to do all those things. We need to stop those things, but just those statements, that's not enough.

Because they focus on the negative and shut down what's possible?

Exactly. If you're going to stop something that people are making a living at, you must replace it with an alternative, right? You have a moral obligation. So we need a politics of yes. In every sentence, and every campaign, every moment, every piece of policy. That's when you'll get folks from all walks of life suddenly showing up. Because we see ourselves in there, in the politics. We want to have solutions.

This shift to the yes, to the what's possible as opposed to what's forbidden, opens up a whole new solution space. That's how you opened up ocean farming as a viable alternative for fishermen. Growing kelp, oysters, out at sea, without fertilizer or other inputs, creating jobs while sequestering nitrogen and carbon dioxide out of the atmosphere. And that's soul filling. Ocean farming, it's the fisherman out at sea in a boat, restoring the ocean, making money. It's about dignity and jobs. But it's not just money. There's a famous story in Newfoundland where they closed down the fishery and they bought everybody's boats and licenses, huge checks. Great money, right? And an old guy gets rid of his boat, buys a brand-new truck. Richer than he's ever been in his life. Every morning, he wakes up at four in the morning, goes down to the docks, and drinks himself to death, wishing he was out at sea.

If we want to fight climate change, we have to get this right and not abandon people like that. This transition to a new climate economy needs jobs with meaning. It is about culture. About soul-filling things. And it's about agency, right? It's not about sitting at home with a full bank account handed down to you from the government. It's having control over your life, building things— building things for your family, building things that make you proud. I think we undervalue the culture of work. A climate-conscious economy has to be an economy that fills the spirit, that's meaningful, that addresses inequality and soulcraft at the same time. Where millions of people head to work every morning filled with pride that they are helping to reimagine and rebuild this country. Without this, you'll never get the politics right. Ever.

Listening to you, you're alluding to a big but subtle class divide in the climate movement, aren't you?

Correct. I don't want to be part of the cubicle class. If that's what the climate movement is offering me, cubicle class and some weird remote farming from my desktop—log on as a robotic boat and a low carbon footprint—I'm out.

This sort of soft class bigotry from government officials, from scientists, from the technology sector—they don't trust, value, or invest in farmer knowledge and innovation. For example, the tech folks love to swoop in to tell us what we're doing wrong as ocean farmers. They are always like, "Let me sell you this sensor or app, and you'll become twice a better farmer."

Explain what's wrong with that?

Look, we need tech innovation, but we also need innovation from the bottom up, where in my experience, there's this wellspring of solutions. One of the biggest problems with our economy is this agency deficit. That you suppos-edly have to be an Amazon to fight climate change. You've got to be an Elon

Musk. But to tackle what lies ahead, we also need to tap into this wellspring of what I call blue-collar and community innovation. Not only because it's there, but we need to bundle solutions. This isn't about one electric truck and going to Mars and a plant burger and a few tech dudes. This is about bundling a thousand solutions together. That's what's going to solve climate change and narrow inequality. We need to bundle.

When you say "bundled solutions," you mean a broad mosaic of community solutions across the entire value chain?

Yes, if we want to address climate change, we can't just invest in kelp biofuels. We don't have the luxury anymore of just focusing on one problem at a time. We need to invest in kelp biofuel and regenerative agriculture, because the kelp should be used in the soil as an alternative to fertilizer. We need to invest in solarizing electric boats and figuring out community models for mobile hatcheries. A broad spectrum of innovation. There's more than one silver bullet. At the same time, we can't just focus on solving climate change. We're not going to get the politics right if we just draw down carbon. Unless we also address inequality, we're building a pathway to failure. So we have to solve for the multiple. And that's messy and complex, but absolutely necessary.

You're bundling a book with many perspectives for a reason, right? This isn't a book about one great hero in history or singular solution. The myth of the individual hero—it's time to dump that. We're still stuck in that sort of Ayn Rand mode of climate solutions. And I think that's a problem. By the way, Ayn Rand used to live right where my farm was. She worked on *The Fountainhead* right at the quarry. One of my life goals is to unravel her impact.

Ha! Well, that's someone to work oneself up against! So let's take that cue, and let's look not at government but at private funders. Investors, impact investors...Impact investing is a big thing. Have you experienced them as helpful?

From my experience, they're too often like, "You got to do one thing. You got to do it well. And it has to make a 10 X return." Packed in there is just this incredible multilevel climate denial in that model. I'm just not convinced that solving climate change needs to be the most profitable opportunity we've ever seen. Do all the climate solutions have to make money? I think that the investment community is in deep climate denial thinking that they can use the twentieth-century business model and return structure to solve climate change. They're just not internalizing the implications of climate change into their investment models.

What I would hope for is that funders embrace more risk and bundle many community solutions together, invest in them. And out of that will emerge our path to building a better world. There's an overlooked important metric, which is when a single solution and its inventor don't matter anymore. Because it has spread, been adapted, modified, the original inventor has become obsolete. If I were a funder, I'd measure and track planned obsolescence.

And perhaps the question is who is making the money, who do you give what stake in the profits. Because when we go to the level of, let's say, the fisherman turned ocean farmer, they are making a living from it.

Yes, exactly. We're just not going to get climate policy through if we build yet another economy based on vertical integration and siphoning off money only to a few men at the top. You're just not going to get social license and social buy-in. It feeds extremism. At the community level, you're going to find a different set of metrics of yes, and of common good: people having profitable farms but also having good healthy food and shared benefits. When people aren't forced to desperately compete, it breeds a different calculus of racial and social justice. Everyone benefiting is a core metric. In my sector it means making sure that beginning farmers can access land, that ownership is horizontal, not vertical, that seed is not privatized, and no one needs to drown in debt. All these pieces matter. The measuring sticks are going to look very different when you pull solutions from the bottom up. If you take all that into account, you are able to retain that sense of meaning that people need and got in the past from fishing or powering the plant. They are going to work every day, trying to solve this, and that solves the climate crisis. They're going to be trying to address irrigation on their farm, and no tilling, and figuring out how to solarize the top of their boat. God, that's a powerful hive mind.

"This is about bundling a thousand solutions together. That's what's going to solve climate change and narrow inequality."

"To tackle what lies ahead, we need to tap into the wellspring of blue-collar and community innovation."

Bren Smith

You've made the conscious decision to open-source your model, your ocean farming know-how. As in, you could have chosen to become the king of kelp, but instead you're choosing to provide a path for as many ocean farmers as possible.

Yes. When folks wanted me to become the king of kelp, I thought about, "Okay, the day I'm going to die, will that feel good? Is that like a good metric?" No! Instead, along with hundreds, thousands of other people, I want to be part of growing regenerative species and regenerative communities. Then I'll die with a smile on my face. There's that piece. The other thing is:

Growing food underwater is so complex. You have so little control: The soil turns over a thousand times a day, you can't see the crops...It's like, you've got no control. And when you don't have control, what you need is as much collaboration as possible.

And that's why open-sourcing is a logical answer.

Yes. The way you get collaboration and ideas is by open-sourcing things, releasing IP. And that comes from a fisherman tradition that whenever you have problems, you get on the radio and call people to find out how to fix them. Now, we have a ten-year period to figure out how to do ocean farming right. And the only way to do that is through open-sourced mass replication—creating networks of learning that transmit really, really fast. That plays out in the GreenWave context in farmer leadership training, where we're doing high-level support of people around the country combined with an online platform.

It allows us to listen to our community and then pump that into our farmer training and just keep circulating that through continually. And that collaborative, open-source, early noncompetitive work has been really, really important. It's funny, at the early stages of growth, the worst thing we could have done in our industry is all creating LLCs and trying to compete against each other. It would have set us all up for failure. Instead, we set up GreenWave as a nonprofit.

Setting up GreenWave as a nonprofit allowed you to be faster because you could share and collaborate from the get-go.

But we also need to move at the right cultural speed in each community. The challenge is we need to move really fast, but in times of transition, process and participation really matter. I learned that out of the cod crisis. Solutions can't just be imposed. Democracy matters more during these times, would be my take. And you know what's interesting?

What?

How that plays out for us on the ground. What that participatory process does in times of crisis. In the ocean world, white working-class fishermen and Indigenous folks have been antagonists for a long time. And there's something really interesting happening now because we're all being impacted very clearly by climate change: New coalitions are forming around our work. Indigenous people are leading our work with Indigenous communities. Dune Lankard is on GreenWave's board, who's also an Ashoka Fellow from Alaska. He said to me, "You're the kind of guy that when I used to walk in the docks and see you coming, I'd turn around and walk away." And now we're working together rebuilding kelp forests throughout the Exxon spill zone. There's real hope there. That alignment, that political realignment. So cool.

Bren Smith spoke with Konstanze Frischen.

Bren Smith is the co-founder of GreenWave. GreenWave's mission is to train and support regenerative ocean farmers in the era of climate change. The organization works with coastal communities throughout North America to create a blue-green economy—built and led by ocean farmers—that ensures everyone can make a living on a living planet. With a low barrier to entry, anyone with twenty acres, a boat, and twenty thousand to fifty thousand dollars can start their own farm.

GreenWave's ten-year goal is to provide training, tools, and support to a baseline of ten thousand regenerative ocean farmers to catalyze the planting of one million acres and yield meaningful economic and climate impacts.

GreenWave's model is deployed for both reforestation—to restore ocean ecosystems and capture blue carbon and nitrogen—and commercial farming, to grow seaweed and shellfish used for food, fertilizer, animal feed, bioplastics, and more.

According to the World Bank, farming seaweeds in less than 5 percent of U.S. waters could absorb ten million tons of nitrogen and 135 million tons of carbon.

When Black Women Walk, Things Change

T. Morgan Dixon

Tapping into the changemaking potential of 1.5 million Black women, T. Morgan Dixon is mobilizing against exhaustion and oppression by fueling a movement that prioritizes joy, health, and self-determination. A conversation about culture change, Black history, the power of self-care, and the radical approach to fighting hatred with hope and love.

Morgan, you co-lead the largest health movement of Black women in America, now a community of over a million and a half women across the country. What does health mean to you and your community?

In some ways, it's a hard question, a layered question. First and foremost, health for Black women in America means not dying. I mean that. Eight out of ten of us are over a healthy weight, and we're dying years, sometimes decades, before we should from preventable diseases like stroke, heart disease, diabetes. The disparities are devastating and have a ripple effect across our families and communities.

On the TED stage in 2017 you said, "the trauma of systemic racism is killing Black women." Why is this happening?

In GirlTrek, we listened to our members, studied the root causes, and created a framework to better understand this question. We call that frame "The Three Deadly I's." Inactivity is the first—it's easiest to see and solve for. Moving your body for thirty minutes every day is the single most powerful health intervention we can do. But when I read statistics like "78 percent of Black women are inactive during leisure time," the question for me is not "Why are Black women inactive?"—it's "What is leisure time?" Most Black women in America don't have leisure time. And that's a labor issue. Black women are busy. Black women are exhausted. Black women are often the sole provider for their families because of systems designed to make it so.

The second "I" is isolation. Research shows that loneliness is deadlier than cigarette smoking. Everyone got a tiny taste of this during COVID. Black women have been isolated for lots of reasons, from zoning and being way out in the suburbs because we can no longer afford to live in our communities—like my mom, who's living an hour away from my sister because there's no affordable housing closer—to things like the prison industrial complex, which has taken away one in three Black men. Or the subsequent policy, that—when your man comes home—doesn't allow him to live in your home if you are in subsidized housing. Those sorts of things have led to isolation.

Last is injustice. 23 percent of Black people in America live in poverty, under the poverty line. We're talking about slave wages for people who are restaurant workers, or caregivers. Injustice also includes toxic runoff in our communities that are too often dumped on. Some are dealing with infrastructure issues that stem from century-old policies that deprioritized investment in Black communities. One of our Trekkers in Denver, she's in a community dealing with toxic runoff. Residents call it "The Swamp." With advocacy training through GirlTrek, in partnership with Stanford University, our member called the city engineers, and they said, "It's a misrouted pipe. It's been there for forty years." So injustice is real. It's not just in Flint, Michigan, although it still persists there. It's all over. These kinds of unfair shakes, especially when they are compounded, are deadly.

These things seem overwhelming. When you look ahead—what are you seeing?

These things are overwhelming. And yet, we see a way forward. It's through collective organizing—the only thing that has shifted culture in the four hundred years that my people have been in America. We've discovered that for us, for Black women, the most seditious acts are actually acts of radical self-care. So we teach women: Give yourself permission to take up space, stop bowing down to oppression, prioritize your health, stop asking permission to show up for the people you care about. It's saying, "Yeah, I'm going to go for a walk at lunch," or "I'm going to take a sabbatical for myself," like the whole GirlTrek team does every year. All of those things together, they allow Black women to live. And if we can eliminate the barriers to health and the systems designed to kill us, we will see the vibrance, bounce-back, and joy that Black women have in abundance—the qualitative side of health.

On that point—in the last year especially, GirlTrek has seen explosive growth in membership. What opportunities for change does this open up?

So, we started with two people in 2010—my college friend and co-founder Vanessa Garrison, and me. And on November 18, 2020, we inspired the one millionth Black woman to join other Black women—to hope together, open their front doors together, step out in faith together, walk in the footsteps of our foremothers who fought for a better world for their daughters and granddaughters. As of June 2021, we are 1.5 million strong. And that's a big deal. That's 8 percent of Black women in America. That makes us finally big enough to effect policy change. We can start to change zoning for corporate pollution, talk to the FDA about how food is sourced at our kids' schools, or even insist on increases in federal minimum wage. And, together, we can create new economies and capital markets in Black communities around wellness. This will be the work of the next ten years, and we're excited about it.

But I can also tell you that our members are not waiting for us to come up with some kind of elegant plan. They're not. They never have. They are doing all sorts of things, every day, to make their communities better, stronger, more beautiful, safer. They are showing that when Black women walk, things change.

An example?

There are hundreds of examples. And because we encourage sharing on Facebook and Instagram, we get to see and celebrate successes across the GirlTrek community. So just the other day on Instagram, I saw that a Girl-Trekker posted a photo of a mural in her neighborhood that she passed on her walk. She tagged the artist, thanked her for beautifying the community, and said that GirlTrek will take care of the street around it. In Atlanta, a whole group of women reclaimed green space. It was a gazillion of them, safely taking care of the trails, leaving no trace, diversifying the parks. We do this in city parks, state parks, regional parks, and national parks. Then in Seattle, a woman launched a search committee for a missing child, the son of a fellow GirlTrekker, and literally just fanned out throughout the streets to find this child after the police had given up on the case…and they found him. So these are a few examples. They leave me wondering often: What would have happened if groups of women had been walking on MaKhia Bryant's block the day the sixteen-year-old girl was killed by police? Walking groups like the ones we're seeing, with this much determination and heart—they are showing how to keep us safe and healthy, keep us moving forward on so many levels.

So, in a sense, you are taking health as a hook, as a starting point for a bigger culture change. Does that help with getting funding?

It's more than a hook, for sure. We need our health, we need to live. But it's true that health is something that can be measured, and that's important

"We will survive. And when we survive, we're going to be intact, and we're going to be intact in a way that still allows us to love you."

"If the civil rights movement were applying for funds today, would anyone fund it? *Did you get justice or peace this quarter, Dr. King?*"

T. Morgan Dixon

for funders and policy makers. You valuing me as human? That's less quantifiable. I mean, if the civil rights movement were applying for funds today, would anyone fund it? I don't know whether Dr. King, Ella Baker, the people of SNCC, the people at SCLC would have been able to fight for their lives and dignity while applying for grant funding and filling out quarterly evaluation forms. *Did you get justice or peace this quarter, Dr. King?* Thankfully, they won, so we have some level of dignity, some rights, our lives, and also a blueprint for allies and funders to see what's possible. And I'm grateful for that, because we do need funding. Not bets of $5 million—we're ready for hundreds of millions, because we have an intervention that works.

And by the way, it saves taxpayers money. The lifetime cost of treating obesity via the healthcare system is, on average, about $13,000 per adult. GirlTrek has our intervention down to $67 per woman. Which would require $67 million dollars to move a million women from inactivity to lifesaving habit formation. And that's not even looking at other effects, like reduced community violence. The future of health care is culture change. And America should invest in proximate leaders with proven track records.

Have you seen the narrative about Black women change over the last couple of years?

Stacey Abrams is following in the footsteps of Fannie Lou Hamer. We've always been awesome. Nothing has changed. You're welcome, America. Ha! Black women are powerful. We're influential. We are a voting bloc. A huge consumer market. And together, GirlTrek will leverage the power of a million Black women to change systems, to protect the environment, to reform criminal justice, to reimagine food systems. We will be at the forefront of a real revitalization of labor law and thinking about the impact of poverty. But we're getting paid sixty-one cents to every white man's dollar. I care more about these issues than how Black women are perceived. I care that Black women are dying disproportionately from maternal health issues that are completely preventable.

The week after George Floyd's murder, you started Black History Boot-camp, *a walk-and-talk podcast that you co-host, where you curate and talk about Black changemakers and history makers whose stories are less well known or celebrated than they should be. Why was this important to do?*

Because our foremothers left a blueprint for changemaking. We needed to remind ourselves that this road ain't nothing compared to the road we have traveled. That ordinary people, like us, being brave alone and working together, have contributed to America in ways that are absolutely critical. From Georgia Gilmore funding the Montgomery bus boycotts with her small business to Richard Allen, the Black founding father, who in addition to starting the AME Church organized citywide frontline responders to save lives all across Philadelphia during a Yellow Fever epidemic. We were able to have truthful and intimate conversations about important strategies for courage and justice. I also love that our allies can listen in and not take up space, and we didn't have to perform under any kind of white gaze because it was just me talking to my friend about the people in history, our ancestors, who continue to instruct and inspire us. Everyone should listen to *Black History Bootcamp*.

I'm always interested in sharing the value of my people outside of the labor we provide—because if our value is only connected to our labor, then we will continue to work ourselves to death. So that's what I do through storytelling—whether it's just us talking now, or if it is us talking on a podcast that a million people download. I think storytelling is powerful enough to change people's hearts and minds.

There's another part of storytelling that's harder. It's reckoning with history that has been hidden from the history books because it's violent, ugly, the opposite of democratic ideals—like the Tulsa Race Massacre that marked its one hundredth anniversary this year. Why is learning these stories important?

So Tulsa, you know, I didn't know the full story until this year. I was grateful for the History Channel documentary that just came out. We did a whole podcast episode on Tulsa, yet somehow I didn't take one moment to think about how it fit into my life. And then, after we got off the podcast with Tamika Mallory as our guest, I was overwhelmed. I took the next day off work, I was so sad. And then I realized why. It's because I know Tulsa. My family's from around there. I grew up with the red dirt of Oklahoma under my fingernails. I needed to know more.

The Tulsa Race Massacre was one of the biggest mass murders of Black people in American history. There were many. Especially in the Red Summer of Hate in 1919. Tulsa is known today because the people there were educated; they ran newspapers, they could tell their own stories. The local papers wrote inflammatory, incendiary articles about the Black population, which led to the racial tension and white lynch mobs. So, in the legacy of Ida B. Wells, I'm committed to telling our history, talking about difficult social justice issues, telling my own family's story, while I'm alive.

I am all for free speech, but if your free speech is destructive or hateful or poisonous to me, my people, and my children, and stokes fear or continues a legacy of white supremacy, you don't have the right to that. There is this arch to today, that people feel really valid in saying completely false things that are just patently untrue. And tolerance for that is credentialing. It has to stop.

Despite all the killings and deaths that happened in 2020, parallel to the podcast, GirlTrek posted positive stories on social media, stories of self-care, self-love. Why was this important to do?

Because rage will kill you. It has killed us. This brings us back to the start of our conversation. The weight Black women carry on their bodies, it is a protection from violence, an attempt to be invisible in a world designed to kill us. So we fight hatred and rage with hope and love. We do. All last year, we were fighting for our sanity, we were fighting for our rest, we were fighting to keep our cortisol and stress hormone levels from spiking. We had to try and create normalcy in a world that is not normal, and we did this by inviting ordinary women to share their extraordinary testimonies.

And so we leaned into hope and we leaned into looking to our foremothers for inspiration, for a blueprint, for a manifesto on how to survive times that don't feel survivable. 2020 was deeply disturbing and violent, and yet still, Donald Trump was no Bull Connor. So, we could at least be as strong as our ancestors. We owe that to them. And that context is empowering. It's like, "We have been here before, and guess what? We survived. And guess what? We will survive. And when we survive, we're going to be intact, and we're going to be intact in a way that still allows us to love you." That's radical.

It is.

It is.

Based on that resilience you just described, what do you see is next in the movement of Black self-liberation, collective liberation?

You know, we did, I think, a good *Black History Bootcamp* episode on A. Philip Randolph. I didn't know that much about him. I knew that he organized the March on Washington, that it wasn't Dr. King. But he also started the first Black union of Pullman porters, the Brotherhood of Sleeping Car Porters, in the 1920s. These were the men who worked the trains, who manned the biggest transportation movement in the free world. With the union, he was able to negotiate in really powerful ways. He's also indirectly responsible for the desegregation of the military. Just fascinating. So when I think about what's ahead, I think about how we can learn a lot from people like A. Philip Randolph, who essentially said: "We control this entire industry. So we can demand respect. And we can shift policy."

Bringing this back to right now, I believe that people like Vanessa and me, people like the founders of Black Lives Matter, those of us who represent a critical mass of Black people, we really have to be at the policy table. We have to look at things as dry as procurement. We have to study collective bargaining. Learn from living legends in the civil rights movement like Angela Davis, who told us that GirlTrek was the revolution, and Marshall Ganz, who is advising our grassroots strategy. So for anyone reading this: We should be at the table.

T. Morgan Dixon spoke with Konstanze Frischen and Amy Clark.

T. Morgan Dixon is the co-founder of GirlTrek, the largest health movement for Black women in America. With 1.5 million members as of June 2021, GirlTrek encourages women to use walking as a practical first step to inspire healthy living, families, and communities. As women organize walking teams, they mobilize community members to support advocacy efforts and lead a civil rights–inspired health movement. Beyond walking, GirlTrek's active members support local and national policy to increase physical activity through walking, improve access to safe places to walk, protect and reclaim green spaces, and improve the walkability and built environments of communities across the United States.

With Partnership for a Healthier America, the Centers for Disease Control, Stanford Prevention Research Center, the American Council on Exercise, Safe Routes to School National Partnership, and the Sierra Club, GirlTrek has developed a world-class training for African-American women to serve as health professionals in the areas of fitness, mental health, nutrition, and environmental stewardship.

You're Welcome: Making Immigration Work

David Lubell

David Lubell has nearly two decades of experience helping cities and towns embrace new immigrants. In this conversation, he shares his lessons from the Trump years, the role that empathy plays in his approach, and why there is often a difference between national populist rhetoric and what is happening at the grassroots level.

David, the movement you founded, Welcoming America, is working on making cities and communities across the United States welcoming to immigrants. Did the impact of your work slow down during the Trump presidency?

No, it did not; it accelerated. Well, let me be more nuanced: During the beginning of the Trump years, in the first year or two, our work in the most conservative places did become a little bit more challenging. But towards the end of the Trump administration, our work was speeding up across the country, regardless of whether counties voted Democrat or Republican. There was a lot of local demand for becoming a welcoming community and making newcomers feel safe and at home. It felt more urgent than ever.

That might be surprising to hear for someone who relied on national news during that time. Why do you think that was the case?

There is a big difference between local and national government—and I believe that is true across much of the world. It is not just a U.S. phenomenon: Look at countries like Poland, Hungary...you have populist national governments, but much less polarization at the ground level. And here in the U.S., well, it was not like the federal government's anti-immigrant rhetoric did not matter at all. But communities and local governments do not simply ride that same populistic wave.

Why not?

Local governments are simply more pragmatic. There are hands-on challenges that need to be dealt with in a timely matter at the local level. Let's say a city government is faced with the fact that the population has been declining for a decade, and the big international company in town is considering moving to a place where its international employees and their families are more supported. At that point, the average local government doesn't focus on national rhetoric about immigrants. Instead, it focuses on the fact that immigrant entrepreneurs are increasing the tax base, adding to the vitality of the place, revitalizing neighborhoods. Local governments live in reality, and that means they're much more likely to be welcoming.

What you condense here are insights that stem from a long process of learning and community organizing.

Yes. It all started in Nashville, Tennessee, where I worked with many others to launch the first Welcoming initiative. In the late '90s, early 2000s, there was a huge growth of immigrant populations across the middle of the U.S. Nashville experienced a large influx of immigrants from Latin America, but also other places—for instance, one of the largest Kurdish populations in the country settled there. And at the beginning, there was a huge backlash. I had founded the Tennessee Immigrant and Refugee Rights Coalition in 2002, organizing for immigrants' rights, and unfortunately the climate for newcomers was headed in the wrong direction. At one point, in 2006, we were trying to fight sixty-five anti-immigrant bills in the state legislature. It was overwhelming. It was at that point that we realized we had to adjust our approach.

Instead of just battling at the legislature, you also started recognizing that there were deeper barriers that needed to be addressed?

Correct. We had to keep trying to prevent the harmful legislation from passing, but we realized we also needed to engage everyday Tennessee residents whose attitudes were feeding these anti-immigrant bills in the first place. We had to reframe the problem.

Expand on that!

Before, we were seeing the problem as the anti-immigrant climate in Nashville and Tennessee, and we were mobilizing against those whose position we did not share, hoping to solve the problem by organizing "our side" against "the other side." Turns out that wasn't sustainable. Instead, we had to address the fears that were motivating the resistance to demographic change, not fight the people who have these fears. And that is true for immigration politics more widely: We cannot "fight" fear of immigrants or immigration. We must address the fear these forces generate. That way, you open up a space of possibilities.

How do you begin such a shift in tactics? By listening? By listening to what actually underpins anti-immigrant sentiments?

Yes. We had to show more empathy for the fears of many long-term residents. Fear is a very human phenomenon. And ignoring it or vilifying it will not stop it from growing. It becomes counterproductive, which is what we were experiencing. It backfires. In our case, we were demonstrating all these good intentions of making Nashville immigrant-friendly, but by fighting those who were struggling with change, we were just driving people further into trying to create an unwelcoming environment.

What did you find out about these fears?

People have different layers of fears. They usually talk about safety, security, and economic —often related to immigrants coming and taking their jobs or sense of safety away. But often underneath all that are cultural fears—that you're being displaced, that you're no longer going to be relevant in your own community, that the dominant language is not going to be your language, and cultural norms are not going to be your cultural norms. That you do not belong or will not belong. And those are deep-seated fears that people don't often understand are happening. They might think it's economic or security fears, and someone might respond with job or crime statistics. But that's not going to do the trick at the beginning, because people's fears go deeper than that. And if that deep level of fear is not addressed, it will metastasize. That was our first learning.

How do you address these fears?

It takes an infrastructure for immigrants and long-time residents to meet and develop relationships, get firsthand information from and about the other side, and see commonalities in practical life. That infrastructure exists in New York or Los Angeles or other traditional immigrant receiving places, because it could develop organically over many decades. People connect with each other in schools and relationships form naturally over generations. But in a place like Nashville, a place without major immigration waves for almost a century, we had to try and speed that process up.

What did you do?

It goes back to community organizing, but organizing intentionally across societal segments. We identified influencers from all the different sectors within the community: from the immigrant and refugee communities, from the established business community, the faith communities, from government. And we brought them together, to basically start to make our way into the different worlds of Nashville. Having coffee and doughnuts after a religious service. Having a barbecue at the community center. All sorts of mechanisms to get people to experience each other in real life. To address that core fear by having immigrants and long-time residents meet one another in a safe environment. To understand that yes, everyone wants jobs and prosperity and a better future for their children, and I know that now not because I'm reading it in some national polling stats, but because I've had a conversation with a Sudanese and a Kurdish and a Mexican parent who is identifying with the exact same dreams I have. The welcoming committee in Nashville was about identifying people that could open new doors for contact and then actually making that contact happen.

Is being welcoming the same as being tolerant?

Good question, and the answer is no: It's more than that. Once fears are addressed and there is a dialogue between immigrants and long-term residents, a new process starts for a community to become actively welcoming. It's based on the same ingredients: bringing the multi-sector coalition back together, including voices of immigrant and refugee leaders, and asking everyone: "How do we reduce all the barriers that are preventing immigrants, refugees, and all residents of the community from reaching their full potential? How do we create structures and policies to change the scenario?"

That's what we did in Nashville, and over time the city started to change. For example, when an English-only referendum was introduced and voted on, it was defeated. A few years prior, it would have easily passed. And once Nashville had proven more resilient to fearmongering, more culturally tolerant, the important work of identifying and changing the institutional barriers to inclusion—in other words becoming actively welcoming—began in earnest and picked up speed over time. So that, over the medium term, the schools became more inclusive and accessible to newcomers, and the same with the social services infrastructure, and other important institutions.

There are national studies that conclude immigrant entrepreneurs create companies at higher level than Americans born in this country, and create more jobs than they take. Are such numbers important in your work?

National statistics don't tend to make much of an impact in a local context, they just don't break through to an everyday citizen. In a city in let's say Ohio, it seems very theoretical when you say immigrants overall in the U.S. add X percent of growth to the national economy. What is much more impactful is when a neighbor tells you that the immigrant owner of that shop in your neighborhood is hiring three more people. In other words, you have to bring it closer to home. We work with communities to create their own verifiable research about local contributions, and almost fifty communities in the U.S. have now done these economic impact surveys, often in collaboration with local universities. So we see, for instance, that between 2013 and 2018, immigrants to Dayton helped strengthen the local job market by helping to preserve or create 3,552 local manufacturing jobs that would have otherwise vanished or moved elsewhere. And they contributed $5.3 billion to the GDP in the region in 2018.

Wow! How important is the economic argument, the fact that immigrants create jobs and pay taxes?

It's very important, of course, but still, it's definitely not everything. Economic data can impact the opinions of some voters, but again you need to address other fears and concerns as well if you want to change the perceptions and actions of the majority.

Economic impact plus organizing—is that when immigration shifts from being seen as a problem to being seen as an opportunity?

For many, yes. And that's the key to scaling it. That's when city rivalry comes in, or should I say "friendly competition." When Nashville was starting to visibly benefit from being a welcoming city, Atlanta or Charlotte went like, "Well, wait a minute. Why aren't we doing that?" And that's exactly how the movement grew. In the northern part of the country, Dayton, that we just spoke about, was key. A local welcoming movement had formed there organically that we connected to. The city of Dayton went all-in on welcoming: They led a multi-sector planning process that led to a road map for change they called Welcome Dayton Plan, they created a Welcome Dayton office within the city, and they advertised their welcoming position to the world. Since then, Dayton has been able to grow its GDP and jobs, and turn around many years of population decline, while simultaneously increasing social cohesion. There are so many other communities in the upper Midwest trying to deal with population decline, so that when Dayton was able to show, "Look, economically we're growing, our tax base is growing, people are moving to Dayton again, and by the way, we created this welcoming Dayton infrastructure," five other communities in Ohio went like, "Wait a minute, we want to do this." And then the mayor of Dayton talks to the mayor of Cincinnati or the mayor of Detroit, and next thing you know, it's really spreading. The Welcoming America movement has grown to over two hundred communities across the U.S., regardless of who's been in the White House. I would go as far as to say that towards the end of the Trump administration, as hostility was growing at the national level, cities—blue and red—leaned in more heavily to counterbalance that hostility at the local level.

Fascinating, right? That there's this level of rhetoric nationally, and then there's a different reality happening on the ground.

Yes. Those winds are very strong at the national level, but at the local level there's a lot of resilience to it.

On the other hand, polarization is real.

Yes, it is real, and it is happening not only around immigration but around a range of issues. But it plays out differently in a specific place. Oftentimes, it is hard for national media to understand the nuances between national and local landscapes. We should have more faith that under the radar and on the ground, there's successful bridging work happening. It's hard to bring a whole country together, but if a community can start to bring its people together, that's important, too, and it is more prone to success.

Talking about voices at the national level—what are the left and right getting wrong?

In general, I would say the left is not empathetic enough to the fears of changing demographics. We spoke about that earlier—if we just vilify people for having fears, we're not going to address the problem. That lack of empathy on the left can be unhelpful. And the right is also lacking empathy and uses immigration as a wedge. If left-leaning politicians can try to convince their voters to vilify those who are afraid of demographic change, right-wing politicians often try to vilify demographic change itself. But as you know, I moved to Berlin, Germany, a little while ago, and I can tell you, many people in Europe are jealous about the U.S. being a country built on immigration. It's something that makes America special; it gives us a built-in advantage globally. And if the far right uses immigration as a wedge, then they are missing a huge opportunity to further the country.

I'm just reflecting on what you said and realizing that these discourses on the right and left tend to be about blaming someone else. And what I hear you saying is that instead of blaming the other, we need to work on changing our own attitude.

Yes, and this is why social change is so difficult. It's not just about changing others, it's also about changing ourselves. It's much easier to try and "improve" someone else, as in "We will give immigrants more English classes and more job training, and that is going to make integration work." I'm not saying English courses are not needed. But if you can for a moment think of an immigrant as a seed planted in a new garden—if you only focus on pouring water on the seed, and not on keeping the soil around the seed fertile, then you won't get very much growth. And unless we just moved from somewhere else last week, where we live we are all part of the soil. And to cultivate the soil it takes a collective approach. That's the hard work, the messy part. For someone on a municipal level, a natural instinct to address immigration might be to read academic papers and then design a policy and put it out in the world. But that's not going to work.

Because it skips the community organizing and engagement piece?

Yes! It's a lot harder to bring all these different sectors together and to organize meetings and listen to and include immigrant and refugee voices. It takes a lot of work. But that's the only way a community is going to create not a bunch of fragmented solutions, but a holistic solution, an infrastructure backed by its residents. And a community needs such an infrastructure to be successful at demographic change. It's a bottom-up approach.

That points to the fact that being a welcoming place is never a fixed status, but a constant process.

Correct. A status that needs to be constantly reaffirmed. But it gets easier once a city gets going. In a community, there's usually 10 percent that are very welcoming anyway, and then there are 10 percent on the other end that are very unwelcoming, hostile towards any immigrants, and hard to move. But in between, there's the 80 percent. Once the shift starts within that group, that's when things move. It doesn't mean there are going to be zero residents against demographic change, but their voices are not going to be the dominant voices anymore. They might have been relatively loud before, but now they are getting drowned out by the welcoming majority. And in the end, being a welcoming city is immigrants and not just about jobs. It's about building social capital, bringing people together so they can hear one another, solve problems together, learn to care about and help each other. It's about creating a safe space so that the unique gifts of every resident can be shared with the entire community. It's about creating a climate that is healthy and fertile, that attracts people. It's about more prosperity and well-being for all.

David Lubell spoke with Konstanze Frischen

David Lubell is the founder of Welcoming America. The organization envisions a world where everyone feels at home. Its mission is to inspire people to build a different kind of community—one that embraces immigrants and fosters opportunity for all. The ultimate goal is to create a tipping point where welcoming communities—ones that are inclusive in policy and culture, and resilient to polarization—become the norm. By changing the narrative, fueling bottom-up movements, and incentivizing local leaders both in the United States and globally, Welcoming America and its Welcoming International program have established a successful track record and foundation for change over the last ten years. Today, the organization's network of leaders for inclusion consists of hundreds of local government and non-profit members from across the U.S., as well as national member institutions supporting bottom-up welcoming movements in Australia, Germany, New Zealand, Mexico, Spain, and the U.K.

Let's Start Where We Agree

Casey Woods

The debate about guns is one of the most polarizing in America. Casey Woods works from within the gun-owning community on making the country safer. A conversation about empathy, pragmatism, fear, and the overlap in motivation that drives both opponents and supporters of firearms.

Casey, you're working with gun owners, and across political aisles, on gun safety. This positions you right in the middle of two opposing viewpoints. How does it feel to be right in the middle?

Well, first off, it's worth pointing out that even the question you just asked—and the words you used—illustrate the point of how difficult it is to work on this issue. The use of the term "gun safety" has become polarizing because it means different things to different sides on this issue.

Ha, I did not know that. I thought I was being sensitive by using the term "gun safety" and not "gun violence."

Well, yes, but nowadays, "gun safety" is also becoming charged. What this illustrates is how sensitive it all is: Even the simplest terminology becomes charged. What "gun safety" means to gun owners is different than what it means to most gun law reform groups. So even your simple question conjured up this whole debate and makes it hard to answer. It feels...well, we're always walking a very delicate line. It is both exhilarating and uncomfortable to be right in the middle with my work. But as the polarization is deepening further, it feels more important than ever to be walking that line.

You said gun safety means to gun owners something that's different from what it means to the other side. What is it?

Well, gun safety for a gun owner who grows up using firearms refers to rules of safe firearms ownership and use. Trigger discipline, muzzle discipline, making sure you're never aiming your gun at anything that you don't want to shoot. There are many rules around making sure that you do not accidentally shoot someone or yourself. Those are the rules of gun safety.

Now, organizations that want to reform legislation have taken the term "gun safety"—because the term "gun control," we all know, is very polarizing—they have taken the term "gun safety" to refer to what they view as new, reasonable laws to govern gun ownership. Different laws. Laws that in turn many gun owners think are unfairly restrictive. And so already that terminology—which seems so bland, right? Everybody wants gun safety—it means two different things to the two different sides.

So language really matters—even in your field.

Yes. One thing I often tell people is: There is no common vocabulary. And that is a real challenge—to not be able to open a conversation without making people feel threatened. Like what you just did. You opened our conversation with all the best intentions, but if you'd said that in a room full of gun owners, it's possible they would have reacted negatively or misunderstood what you meant, even though you would have had the best intentions. And that makes it really hard—when there is no common language to begin with.

So how do you handle that?

We get really specific. We don't talk about being a gun violence prevention organization anymore. We say precisely what we do—we work from within the gun owner community to prevent gun suicide and gun homicide. Why is that? Because many gun owners would disagree with you if you said suicide is gun violence. For them, gun violence is criminal activity, which has nothing to do with how they handle firearms. They don't see suicide as "gun violence." In the past, suicide carried huge stigma—the phrases "commit crime" and "commit suicide" are similar. And because of that association, I have stopped saying "committing suicide," because in the ears of gun owners it sounds too close to saying "committing a crime."

So what do you say?

I say "died by suicide."

Ah.

So it's little things like that, that even years into my work, I modify. Right now, there are many people who want to convince gun owners that gun suicide should be considered gun violence. My point is, gun owners die by suicide at higher rates than others and many of them don't want it to be called "gun violence." So why spend our time trying to convince them of this terminology? Let's just call it "gun suicide" and work with them on it. Listen to what your audience tells you. That is so important. If a terminology is not working for gun owners, then we're going to change it and we're going to focus on what works.

You learned that in a very personal way. You grew up in a gun-owning family.

Yes, I grew up in a big gun-owning family in Arkansas. Everyone hunted, and half of my family was a farming family until my dad's generation. And so growing up around guns, firearms...They represent a sense of independence. They represent an ability to put food on the table, the ability to protect yourself and your family. That is something that gets lost in this debate about guns and firearms: the protective motivations that inform why the majority of gun owners own guns. It is not surprising why in the last year, and including now, there have been record-breaking numbers of gun sales—I mean, they just went through the roof.

Because people feel the need to protect themselves?

Right. Even many people who never before thought they were going to buy a firearm bought one, including a rise in gun ownership in communities of color. In times of uncertainty, increasingly, many people feel like they can't rely on the police or anyone else to protect them.

I can follow.

Now, what folks tend to do is to debate this fact. They argue: "Well, I don't think buying a gun or not buying a gun is what people should do." But in my view, it's more productive to focus on the motivation. It is very powerful and important.

The motivation that I want to protect my family?

Yes! Everybody wants their families to be safe. For some people that means fighting for a world where there's no guns. For some people that means buying a bunch of firearms and going to the range three days a week. It's exactly the same motivation. It's the same motivation, love and fear for our family, that makes people fall on opposite ends of the spectrum. So tapping into those protective motivations to find out places that we have in common and can make progress on—that is really core to overcoming polarization. We need radical empathy with all sides.

Would you say progressives are lacking empathy for gun owners? And vice versa: Aren't conservatives lacking empathy, too?

I always encourage people on all sides to focus on the motivations behind people's choices—on both sides. That is, for me, part of my definition of having radical empathy. I think many people on the progressive side don't understand what drives most gun owners to own and carry guns. As I said: gun owners cite personal and family protection is their number one motivation. Their point of view is: "I'm not waiting around for someone to come protect my family—I protect them." There is a sense of duty there.

Often, I don't think that version of their motivations gets accurately portrayed in the media—you're always seeing extremes. I work with two of the biggest chapter-based gun-owner groups in America. And they are all about education and responsibility. They meet monthly. Every weekend they have events, they train people. They are taking safety very seriously. They invest a lot of their time into these things.

Also, the sort of profile of the gun owner is not always that stereotypical middle-aged white guy. We work with the biggest group of gun owners of color in America, and they have had skyrocketing membership and more interest than ever before. Post–George Floyd, post–Ahmaud Arbery, their question has become more and more urgent: "If something bad were to happen, am I going to call the police? What do I need to do if I can't call the police? How do I protect myself and my family?" For many of them the answer has been to buy a gun.

And what do you wish gun owners had more empathy for when it comes to the other side?

Applying the same: asking and understanding what is someone's motivation. If you're terrified that your child's going to get killed in a school shooting, that is a very understandable and powerful motivation. I often point out what I think is the biggest dividing line between the two sides on this issue: Do you believe guns make you more or less safe? Your answer to that question defines your response on this issue. But at the end of the day, the things that drive us are the same, so let me repeat it again: Everybody's operating from a place of love and fear. We love our families. We love the people in our lives, and we want to protect them. And we're afraid. Fear is a very powerful motivator, too.

And it can be odd to me sometimes that gun owners don't understand that if guns are scary to you, then of course you're going to say that we should have less of them. Everyone's trying to move towards what they think is a safer world for their families.

So when you tap into that motivation, the desire to protect our family, the motivation of love and fear...what becomes possible?

The average gun owner wants to save lives, so if we focus on giving them ways to do that, we can shift outcomes. Here's an example: Suicide prevention is a huge part of our work – we were talking about suicide before. A fact that most people don't know: Two-thirds of gun deaths in America are suicides. That means that two-thirds of all gun deaths are gun owners killing themselves. It's a brutal truth, one that shocks people, because suicide is not covered in the media the way mass shootings are. Even many gun owners don't know that statistic. The reality is that gun owners aren't more likely to attempt suicide, they're just more likely to die, because guns are deadlier than all other suicide methods combined.

Now—knowing that the motivation of the average gun owner is wanting to save lives, our answer to the suicide statistic is to empower gun owners with new norms and practices that help them save friends and family members from gun suicide. We empower them to intervene to hold onto or secure guns until a crisis has passed. Essentially, we're building the "Friends Don't Let Friends Drive Drunk" model, except instead of alcohol and cars, we're talking about firearms and suicide. And we do it in a way that is in-your-face and a bit irreverent, because conversations about guns and suicide are complicated. The call to action on the Overwatch Project, our veteran suicide prevention program, is "Just Fucking Ask." It really breaks through the noise and gets veterans to pay attention in a different way.

That sounds pragmatic.

Another area we work in is preventing the illegal flow and use of guns—the

> "Everybody wants their families to be safe. For some people that means fighting for a world where there's no guns. For some people that means buying a bunch of firearms and going to the range three days a week."

Casey Woods

kind that drives gun homicide. One thing many people don't know is that around 400,000 guns are stolen from individual owners every single year.

Gun theft is one of the top sources of guns used in crime. Even though gun owners are deeply concerned about crime, they are inadvertently and involuntarily arming the people committing the crimes they fear. But no one wants their guns to be stolen and be used to harm someone.

Many gun owners simply weren't aware of how big a problem gun theft is. So again, we focused on how we can give them new ways to prevent crime and save lives. We created a campaign and curriculum on gun theft prevention that is now being used all over the country. I mentioned the chapter-based groups we work with? They have thousands of members in virtually every state. This past year, hundreds of their chapters taught our theft prevention program to their members. The average gun owner is very focused on preventing crime—that's why they own a gun, right? So here we are giving them another way to do that.

It might feel like a weird niche—I mean, who thinks about gun theft as a driver of crime? But if we can get every gun owner to be aware of that fact, and take steps to protect their guns from being stolen, it will have a significant impact on crime.

The two examples you gave us—theft prevention and suicide prevention— are they chosen on purpose by you because they are not politically loaded?

Yes. So many gun related issues are so deeply politicized, that in our work, we purposefully focus on spaces that are perceived as non-political. Generally, when politics are on the table, things get difficult. From the experience of my work, there's been such scorched earth on these issues politically that it will be very difficult to bring people together around it.

I mean, there's a lot of competition, but in my opinion, gun policy is the single most polarizing issue in America, as you said in the beginning. In many elections, the most accurate predictor of how someone is going to vote is whether or not they live in a home with a gun. And thus, gun ownership has become something of a political football. I'm not saying we shouldn't be fighting policy battles. I'm just saying after years and years and years of this, it really makes it difficult to even have a conversation.

How can you make progress when so many subjects are basically untouchable?

It matters how you work. We're really focused on a collaborative process. When we're building a new initiative, we bring together people and groups to contribute to its creation. If you bring in a collaborative process, give people an opportunity to be part of it, to contribute to it, to feel ownership, you can move ahead in a different way. Those chapter-based gun owner groups I mentioned? Well, we brought them in on the ground floor when we were creating projects. And once we have built an initiative, our big focus is on growing partnerships. Our informal motto is "It's not about us." The focus must be on empowering leaders who are closest to the issue, on empowering networks. Take it, go with it. You lead. You teach it, you take it, you own it. What do you need from us to lead on this? That's our role. It's not to be the leader in every space. It's to give other leaders, who are closest to these issues and communities, what they need to be able to lead effectively.

I'm wondering with that approach in mind, where you think there is space for political breakthroughs. You said before, look, we need to take the political out of the gun debate. But if you were to engineer a plan, to advise the government, where would you go?

Oh, I have ideas. If I could wave a magic wand and say, "This is what I want you to pass," I would want to get folks to pass initiatives that put real resources behind suicide prevention programs that are community-based and that promote education, building new norms, with gun owners in the lead. We should put resources behind that. There are a lot of resources put behind legislation called "red flag laws"—laws that allow police or family members to petition a state court to order a temporary removal of firearms from a person who may present a danger to others or themselves. For many gun owners, red flag laws can feed the narrative that someone's trying to take people's guns away, right? At a moment when people are in crisis, it can create a lot of fear. And so it's dangerous to have that be presented as the first or only solution on the table for people who are afraid a friend or family member might attempt suicide. I would love to see even greater resources invested in collaborative programs that educate gun owners and empower them to intervene, to prevent suicide in their own communities.

The equivalent that I always draw on is again the "Friends Don't Let Friends Drive Drunk" model that we touched on earlier when we spoke about suicide prevention. If the only message for that campaign had been "Call the cops to have them take away your friend's keys when they are drunk!" nobody would have done it. The message was instead: "You, the friend who loves this person, talk to them in a loving way about holding on to their keys when they are drunk and can't drive." And with that, it's become probably the single most successful peer-intervention campaign in history. So—let's learn from it, and empower organizations that work with gun owners to spread this message!

Give me an example that illustrates how this works.

I've got a lot of them, because this peer-intervention approach is at the core of our suicide prevention work. We have a few short films that highlight these stories. A really powerful one to me is that of a veteran named Jay, whose dad was a Vietnam veteran. Jay's dad lost his first wife to suicide. And then

Jay went off to war and came back with post-traumatic stress. Then, one night, Jay had a call with his best friend, a fellow veteran—and two hours later, his best friend killed himself. Jay hit rock bottom—but his dad was there. He told Jay, "I can't stand to lose my son. I lost my first wife. I can't lose my son." From then on out, they had a deal: If Jay was struggling, his dad would hold on to his firearms until the crisis passed. He saved Jay's life. And now Jay does that for other veterans—if they are having a hard time, he will step in and talk to them and hold on to their guns temporarily. Jay is passing this new norm forward in his community of friends.

That's the power of surfacing the hard things. Somebody at the beginning of that chain, in this case his dad, was willing to have a difficult conversation, and that has ended up saving not just his son's life, but other people's lives. That is something that we try and build on. And to focus on positive examples. Where's the success? On all these issues that we work with, there's such a negative narrative so much of the time. Instead, let's lift up the people that are having the impact that we want to see and allow people to learn from that.

If I wanted to have difficult conversations with others around political issues we passionately disagree over...what would you recommend I do? What values should underpin these conversations?

Look, radical empathy is huge, at least in my work. When possible, go in with a nonjudgmental view and an open mind. Be conscious of that, always. Many of us probably agree on 80 percent of things, but it is the 20 percent that trigger us and make a conversation impossible.

Mm, that's probably something I could indeed benefit from – focusing on the commonalities.

Yes, that's another thing I wish I could wave my magic wand over and it would be the norm. And it brings me to another value: Collaboration. That is really important on polarizing issues. We bring a lot of people to the table from the very beginning of all of our initiatives. I call it "the power of the half-baked idea." It's harder to be successful when you go to people and say, "I've got this all figured out. We want to do X, Y, and Z. Can you come in and be part of this piece?" People don't feel like they are part of the process.

Instead, we say, and mean it: "This is wide-open. Come participate in this process. You can own it. And you are the experts."

We're starting such a collaborative process now on a new initiative around Black teen suicide—it has risen dramatically in the last decade. And in the last two years, nearly half those suicides have been with firearms. That's a new phenomenon, because suicide has historically been lower in the Black community. So the numbers, the rising numbers of Black teens dying by suicide, are shocking when I share them. Like I said before, over the last several years we have partnered with organizations for gun owners of color. So now I'm at the very beginning of this process where I'm just calling people and saying, "Do you want to come be part of this project and help create it—because you are the experts." That collaborative approach requires humility and trust. And if we could bring more of that to a lot of issues, then I truly believe that we would be more successful in solving big problems.

Casey Woods spoke with Konstanze Frischen.

Casey Woods is the founder of FORGE. FORGE is the only national nonprofit specifically focused on working from within the gun-owner community on transformative, nonpolitical efforts to prevent gun suicide and gun homicide. Two-thirds of gun deaths are suicides, and FORGE's suicide prevention initiatives include the Overwatch Project, which empowers gun owners, starting with the veteran community, to intervene with friends and loved ones to prevent suicide through protective firearm storage measures. FORGE is also developing suicide prevention initiatives focused on gun owners of color and women gun owners.

FORGE's other projects include the Firearms Security Alliance, a collaborative, partnership-based initiative that unites gun owners, gun groups, ranges, firearms instructors, law enforcement, and other community leaders to work together to prevent the illegal flow and use of firearms. The Firearms Security Alliance's first campaign is focused on gun theft prevention: More than 400,000 guns are stolen from individual owners every year, and those illegally obtained firearms fuel crime. FORGE's national Firearms Security Alliance partners include chapter-based gun-owner groups that represent more than 50,000 actively engaged members nationwide.

Through these initiatives, FORGE is tackling the root causes of 97 percent of gun deaths.

We See What We Look For

Trabian Shorters

Why Asset-Framing matters: Trabian Shorters unveils how popular narratives have contributed to upholding racial hierarchies by characterizing Black people and communities almost exclusively in stigmatizing ways, and why the time is ripe for change. A conversation about the opportunity that opens up for America when we define people by their aspirations and contributions before noting any challenges.

Trabian, you wrote a great article a few years ago called "You Can't Lift People Up by Putting Them Down" about how philanthropy unintentionally causes harm to communities when it defines them exclusively in stigmatizing ways. When did you start thinking about this?

That article grew out of my work with the BMe community, the network I founded of Black community leaders, champions, and innovators. And BMe grew out of the recognition that the brothers and sisters that I grew up with may have been poor, they may have been living in a Black sort of stereotype community with low employment, high crime, etc. But what I knew firsthand was that 90 percent of them were just trying to live and make things better for themselves and others. It was just super normal. And I realized that part of our Black narrative, the 90 percent of our story, gets totally ignored—as if it doesn't exist.

Ignored how? Can you give an example?

Well, we see reports about Black communities that say things like for instance, "Black males don't volunteer for mentoring programs." Which, okay, may be technically, statistically true based on the findings in a survey. But that's because the survey asked the wrong question. Because brothers mentor other kids all the time. We mentor cousins, nephews, we mentor family friends' children. We create basketball leagues and baseball leagues just for the sake of having the kids under our care for periods of time, so we can teach them values. What I'm saying is that Black men have more integrated and effective ways of mentoring than these formal mentoring programs offer, so we don't sign up for them. But that gets translated as we're not volunteering, when in fact we often do far more than most mentoring programs—so why sign up for something less natural and less relational?

And so at some point, I just realized that we're leaning our ladders up against the wrong narrative. That's what I mean when I say you can't lift someone up by putting them down. We see what we look for. So I asked myself, "Well, what if we look for something different? Could we see that, too?" And it turns out that yes, we can. And we must.

In other words, look for what's working, not what's broken?

Correct, that's where you start. But the assumption in social impact circles is "let's fix problems by fixing the ones closest to them, who we describe in terms of deficits." That assumption really should be challenged—because it inclines you towards stigmatizing people, and towards exerting control and imposing metrics that focus on deficits that might not even be there in the first place—as in the mentoring example. Like I said, you can't lift people up by putting them down. You've got to pick them up by lifting them up. Equity itself is always, always a concept related to value. Financial equity, social equity—we're always talking about what and who is valuable. And you can't start a value conversation by pointing out costs, or alleged failures. Let's start the equity—the value—conversation with how someone, or a community, is specifically an asset and of value, then we can talk about how to build on those strengths.

I do Asset-Framing workshops, and one of the exercises I sometimes include is a game on stigmatizing people. It's hard to describe without getting into the whole exercise, but the point is that the stigma game lets people experience how quickly they can be made to feel less agency, less confidence, less engagement. It's like, "Okay, so that's what happened to a room full of accomplished professionals within two minutes. So, for Black people who are forced to live this way their whole lives, can you imagine?" These folks are not less capable. But they're living under a different narrative, a narrative of stigma, and they experience stigmatizing responses that come from it.

How does the narrative of brokenness get reinforced?

Well, here's a typical way: If you're a Black kid raised like me, your guidance counselor in high school will encourage you to tell a story about your horrible background to get scholarships. That will absolutely happen. So that negative narrative ends up becoming "your" story, your agency. And people learn to identify themselves as "I'm from the hood. I overcame XYZ." Or whatever it is. They introduce themselves that way not because it's really what defines them but because that's how society is willing to see them. If they don't say these things, then they literally become invisible, right?

The same kind of things play out in organizations. Way too many Black organizations have learned to survive by running down the faults and challenges and stigmas of Black people because it's what funders want to hear. And so that's how we live. We live by denigrating our people in the name of helping them. So any victories we secure, we secure by writing our people into the public consciousness as a problem. It's absurd. Deficit-framing your people, even when you win, you lose.

How do you flip this narrative?

It starts with recognizing that all of us have a story in our head about who we are, and we try to live into that narrative, whatever it is. We do that on an individual basis, and we do that on a national basis. And if we tweak that story—or more accurately, a person's sense of identity, their role in the story—then that influences related activities. Because the identity that we carry has an outsized influence on our behavior. Asset-Framing is about defining people's identity by their assets, by their aspirations, by their contributions. By what they are good at and what they aspire to become. Once you adopt that perspective, you'll see totally different options. A much fuller spectrum of possibility.

For instance, BMe Community is built upon Black leaders who have earned the trust of their communities—innovators, community builders, authors, business owners, etc. Some have served time in prison and found their way to a new life, and now they are helping others do the same. No one hides their past in any way, but no one leads with the least empowered aspect of their life either. That's intentional. Because when it comes to narrative change, it's not a matter of what people call you. It's always about what names you answer to. If somebody calls you a bad name, that's on them. If you respond and play into that, well, that's on you, right?

So, BMe Vanguard Fellows are answering to different names. They are coming together around the next narrative for Black America that leaves behind the association with brokenness, so we can legitimately claim our right as free people in this democracy. I mean, Black folks have been contributing to liberty and justice for all since longer than this nation had a name. We fight for it. We fought for it in the last election, in case you weren't paying attention. So, for us to pretend like we are guests in the nation that we built is absurd, right? Even so, being champions of America's highest values doesn't

"You can't lift people up by putting them down. You've got to pick them up by lifting them up."

"Human beings literally all want the same things. We just have these narratives that tell us who deserves them and who does not."

Trabian Shorters

mean we are beneficiaries of those same ideals. America hasn't gotten there yet because they ignore that narrative of who we have always been here.

How is philanthropy responding to Asset-Framing?

We train big foundations to adopt, or at least explore, Asset-Framing—to give you a basic simple example, what happens if instead of your grant application beginning with "problem statement," it began with "your aspirations for this project"? I recognize that people are going to engage this asset narrative from their perspective, and I don't assume everybody is going to take all the lessons from it that I would take, or that BMe leaders would take. Some foundations call us in because they are basically worried, as in: "How do we make sure that we don't say the wrong thing?" But my favorite group is the C-suite folks who are plain tired of the old stuff. They come in saying, "We've got to do something different." They take the tools we give them, and they do things like change their mission statement. They get together and create whole new foundations. I know for a fact that Asset-Framing has led to at least two and a half billion dollars in private money being committed to philanthropic and for-profit investing initiatives that benefit Black people and apply an asset lens. So I know those kinds of measurable material resource flow changes are happening. I also know that in people's heads, how they think about each other is changing, which I think might be even more important.

Changing how?

Cognition is a human thing. When we learn to identify each other by our aspirations and contributions, we literally see our commonality more easily that way. Asset-Framing reminds folks that poor people aspire, too. Poor people make contributions, too. Being at the "bottom of the pyramid" doesn't mean that you don't have values, it just means that you've got a lot of unearned obstacles, right? And so when people can honestly, sincerely recognize the aspirations and the contributions of everyone, they understand how much overlap there is. Human beings literally all want the same things. We just have these narratives that tell us who deserves them and who does not. But we all deserve them. It's a matter of seeing it that way.

What I'm getting at is that the way many of us are taught to engage with social impact primes us to be disingenuous, not because our intentions are insincere, but because of the way philanthropy is set up. You're speaking about groups of people with language you would never use to their face. You're using words like "disadvantaged" and "at-risk," etc. Asset-Framing, on the other hand, is an invitation to use the exact same words in a grant proposal, a policy proposal, that you use when speaking to people face-to-face. "Hardworking," "aspiring," "striving," etc. Like one voice, right? Then what you see about them and what you feel about them ends up being very, very genuine.

You were a journalist early in your career, also a best-selling author. Do you see journalists as allies in changing the narrative?

Yes, absolutely. And we're collaborating with partners like Solutions Journalism Network to help newsrooms, editors, and reporters do rigorous reporting with an asset frame. What does that look like? It looks like telling the whole story of communities and communities of color—the story of what's not working and the story of what they're doing about it. How do you do it? Start with the recognition that people want to care for their children, create businesses, and live in great communities. Then the story you end up telling is about "Well, what is obstructing that? Why is it so hard for them to do that?" And those tend to be stories about policies that systematically impoverish. Leaders made decisions to let the pipes in Flint be toxic. These are not accidents of nature. And so when you talk about the decisions that are making it harder for real people to realize their worthy aspirations, well then people say, "Oh, well, we've got to change those systems." Not just make it so that people can survive under those systems.

How does this focus, and a narrative shift around Black people, interact with our moment in America?

The context BMe is bringing to this conversation is that we are right now living out the last generation of white majority in the United States. Since its founding, the country has had a white majority. But the generation of Americans that has no racial majority is already in school. You and me, we're living out the last days where "majority rule" and "white rule" are synonymous. This means we're entering a moment where we can no longer propagate certain myths and deficit frames, because the new mainstream will challenge them. The mainstream of Black and Brown and white and Asian, right? They'll challenge them because they won't feel true to their experience.

So we're finally at a point where our democracy will either learn about pluralism, or it will fail. People with genuine disagreements will have to learn how to sort them out, or the democracy will devolve into something else. And as we can see, that's not a given, right? I bring all this up to say I understand why so many people think about this as a Black/white sort of racial thing. But it's bigger than that. It's the ideal of a society where majority rule is a shared concept. The majority is becoming a racial mix, no longer a prime race. And for that democracy we've all got to learn new skills.

Are you hopeful Americans can learn these new skills, new values?

I think the transition is going to be painful, unfortunately. We're going to stumble and we're going to hurt each other, and we're going to dredge up things that we didn't know, didn't want to know. That's where these pluralistic values become very important. We'll need to be able to recognize that when someone lashes out, they're doing so out of pain. They might be trying to hurt you, but they're doing it out of pain. Not really or not usually out of any rational disdain for you. For a person, for any of us, to be able to understand this and still operate requires a kind of maturity that most of us haven't been taught.

On issues of race in the United States, I think the biggest clash perhaps that's going to come up is the clash between Black organizers and some white liberals. Because even our allies rely on the deficit narrative. I don't know how many times I've seen really sincere white folks who think that it is a good idea to surround themselves with pictures of Black children that they're helping, "saving." Black people get tired of it and wonder why they can't be seen another way—just as capable humans? And it's because we don't yet have a common narrative that supports that. The thing is, if your opponents practice the sociopathy called "white supremacy," then you expect that denigrating relationship. But when you get it from your friends, you develop resentment. From a meta structure, there's very deep frustration of Black leaders with white liberals. And what's interesting about that is if you've ever read any of Martin Luther King Jr.'s writings, he voiced it very clearly, too.

Can we use Asset-Framing for the collective, for all of us in the U.S.?

In BMe fellowships we often discuss "If Asset-Framing is right for you, well then what about America? Should America also be defined by its aspirations and contributions before we get to all the problems?"

If we can hold space long enough to define this country by its highest aspirations, then when the betrayals of those ideals are aired, the wrongs are heard, and the denials have been relinquished—then it becomes much easier to see that we're in this boat together. We all want the highest aspirations, "liberty and justice for all," to be true. And how we respond to this moment determines whether we finish the journey, or whether we give up and turn our democracy into something that is not truly democracy. Choosing to Asset-Frame is our best way forward, because I don't think it's a given yet which way we as a people will go.

Trabian Shorters spoke with Konstanze Frischen and Amy Clark.

Trabian Shorters is the founder of BMe Community. BMe is an award-winning community of Black leaders, builders, and their allies who work to expand freedoms to Live Own Vote and Excel in America. BMe's mission is to build more caring and prosperous communities inspired by Black people. Trabian Shorters created and owns the cognitive framework called Asset-Framing®, and BMe Community is the leading provider of Asset-Framing® training to senior executives of major foundations and social enterprises.

"Poor People Are Not Charity Cases"

Mauricio Lim Miller

Based on his own life experience, Mauricio Lim Miller argues against well-intended poverty reduction approaches led by people with an underlying class bias. In this conversation, he explains why people considered poor are the experts of their own lives, why so much goes wrong when we treat them differently, and how to overcome a class divide that is compounded by race and gender.

Mauricio, you've written a book with the tagline "Most of what you believe about poverty is wrong." It's also a very personal book, because it draws on the experience of your family as Mexican immigrants to the U.S.

Yes. As a child, I came to San Jose with my mother and my sister, and we lived there and different parts of Northern California. I grew up in Spanish-speaking neighborhoods that I'd come to know later people would think of as poverty neighborhoods. They did not present to me like that. To me, I always lived in an amazing place. My neighbors were folks who were working really hard, two jobs, three jobs, and struggling, yes, struggling a lot. But people were resourceful and community-oriented and hardworking and funny.

When did it strike you that not everyone would see your neighborhood like you did?

The extent of the discrepancy I realized only when I went to Berkeley. I was the first in our family to go to college, and with that, I entered this other world. And it was stunning: While I was on campus, I got treated different-ly. People figured I was a student and assumed I must be smart. And they behaved respectfully. But when I would take the Greyhound bus back to Sacramento, where my mother lived at the time, on the way to my neigh-borhood, folks would look at me and they'd treat me as if I was dumb. It was just really interesting how people interacted with me in these two different environments, given what they picked up as the stereotype.

The women in your family play an important role in your book—and in your life, I should add!

Yes. First, there's my mom. A single Mexican mom. She moved us to the U.S. because she believed that in this country, we'd have a chance to be viewed more by our merits, by what we'd build up, rather than our roots. She only had a third-grade education in Mexico, but she was very smart, resourceful, and an amazing seamstress and designer. Now, we were poor, but she came here not because she wanted welfare support. She wasn't looking for any-thing like that. In fact, help programs insulted her.

And I'm assuming gender and race stereotypes weighed on her in addition?

Yes. And naturally, she hated those openly racist and sexist. But she had perhaps more trouble dealing with the more liberal. Though she tried to hide our economic status, in her church she was looked upon as "needy," which to her translated to "weak." She was anything but weak! The paternalism of offers of help drove her nuts. "They take my pride away," she used to say. "I can work as hard as anybody else. I'm as smart as anybody else. I don't need special programs." I think that's what really irritated her the most. She just wanted to feel included, instead of being treated as a charity case.

And your sister?

My sister became pregnant at sixteen, and the guy she married took her off to New York, where they had three kids. She was treated like a poor mom who was in trouble. My sister is really smart and hardworking, and she would be a great manager and supervisor, but nobody saw her that way. Her name is Raquel, but she changed her name to Rachel, to hide the Mexican part. So I grew up with these two women who worked harder than me, were more resourceful than me, were smarter than me, and didn't have a chance.

Your mother's and sister's examples influenced your decision to work on poverty alleviation.

Yes. I had made it through Berkeley and had become an engineer—that's what my mother had dictated [laughs]. There was no choice—sacrifices were made for me, and therefore, I should become an engineer with a solid income. But when I lost my mother in my midtwenties, I decided to join the nonprofit sector. To join the war on poverty. That's what it was framed like in the late '70s. Everyone was forming a nonprofit; funding shifted in that direction. We all thought we could change the world.

But you soon felt you weren't?

Right. The short of it: I quickly realized that while I was managing this big nonprofit that was running big programs to help poor people—at one time I had a staff of 120!—I realized that I wouldn't bring my own nephew and nieces through my own services! At that time, they were going through as much trauma and adversity as my nonprofit clients; they were right in the target group. Yet I knew I wouldn't bring them through my services. And that was such a paradox! Because our nonprofit was considered to have some of the best services in the country. We were a nationally recognized model. Bill Clinton invited me to the State of the Union address because of my work. And that's when it all dawned on me: This poverty alleviation business is not working. If my organization is supposed to be among the best of the country, then something here must be just fundamentally wrong.

What had made you see differently?

The experience of being in a different class. Now that I was middle income, I got treated differently—similar to the Berkeley "aha" moment, but more far-reaching. There was a whole class of services available to me and my new peers—counseling, therapy, financing, drug rehab. Middle-class people need all the services poor people need, but for the middle class and upwards, the system is demand driven. It is driven by what the client wants. That's fundamentally different from what poor people get. For them, there's no demand-driven service. It's program driven. Or actually, for me at the time, it was driven by whatever I could get funding for. Poor clients had to fit my funding criteria. And in order to be eligible, they had to look needy. They had to portray themselves as somebody who was very weak and needed to be saved. That's what really pleased the program, because then we could go to the funder and show off: "Look at these poor people. Without us, they couldn't have made progress, so you have to fund us, the professional intermediary, the expert."

That would have made your mother run away screaming.

Exactly! My mother hated it when people would treat her as a charity case. When they would offer her little bits of money, that would offend her the most. That perspective was really mind-blowing for me, and it still really bothers me—because I also feel tempted to give away a little money and feel good about myself and not have to worry about poor people. However, my mother's perspective was that this was an easy way out: Do a little good, buy off your guilt, and move on. Poor people just want to be included in the system as equals, based on merit. But that option wasn't available to her.

I'm reminded of a thread I read on social media the other day, where people were sharing what they thought counts as classy when rich, and trashy when poor. And one answer was: bilingualism.

Ha, see? It's because of that, that's why the book was subtitled *Most of What You Believe About Poverty Is Wrong*. We have so many preconceived assumptions from our viewpoint as being privileged...Because of this class difference, we will never truly understand the other side, and that is of course compounded by race and gender. The dilemma ends up being the following: If you're not the expert, then why are you the one getting the funding? If poor people are the experts of their own lives, then they're the ones that can come up with the best solutions. They're the ones that actually can figure out the steps that are necessary, what the balance has to be in their life. If they are the ones that can solve it, why doesn't the funding go to them? Why don't we talk with them?

Are you arguing for some sort of universal basic income here?

That's not the point I'm trying to make. Like I said, my mother would really get upset if people offered her little bits of money. Universal basic income and help from above—it's all nice, but it's like charity. It's not that my mom didn't need the money. But it did not fundamentally change her class and race status. And that's what anti-poverty efforts should be about. It is about changing status.

And for that, you need more than money?

Correct. You need your own networks of people and the strength of the community, and the same dignity and respect. Take my sister: When her husband would beat her up, she didn't go to the nonprofit that ran some program. She went to her friend's house. The strength of social networks helps you get through racism, sexism. It helps you emotionally. That mutuality within a community is the factor that anti-poverty programs tend to overlook. They promote a relationship back to the social worker. They don't promote the relationship between families.

How can this mutuality be leveraged against poverty?

What really impacts people is their peers. Sometimes out of jealousy, sometimes envy...the fear of missing out. My mother would look around the neighborhood and she'd come home and say, "Oh, so-and-so was able to get their kid into college!" That was the deepest influence you can get. Peer-driven networks inspire.

But how do you operationalize this?

I started an organization to reinforce existing peer ties of mutuality among poor families, many of them immigrant families—a kind of anti-program. It was one of our principles we would not interfere and prescribe our clients what to do, and any staff who'd be seen helping the families in this way would be fired. To tell you how difficult that was, here's a story: Not long after we introduced this principle of not helping in a traditional way, we're getting a call from one community member, and she says: "I just got in a car accident, and the insurance company is coming after me and the bank is coming after me. Could you refer me to legal aid because I need a lawyer?"

Now, that's a relatively simple ask...

Yes, in many ways, not a big deal—except that I had just told my staff that if they interfere, if they help, they'll get fired. So we put this lady on speakerphone and ask her if there's anybody in her network that has had an accident and used a lawyer, and could they refer her to that lawyer? The woman thought for a minute, and said: "No." So we follow our pro-tocol and ask her: "Okay, so then, has anybody that you know ever used a lawyer that they really like?" The woman thinks about it and thinks and then says: "No." At that point, my staff and I are looking at each other and I'm thinking, "Oh my, I might have to give approval to break the principle...It's just about a phone number, after all."...When suddenly the lady breaks in: "Oh, I babysit for an attorney! Should I ask her?" And we go, "Yes!" And then the woman remembers that the attorney has mentioned she is feeling guilty because she keeps coming home late, keeping her at work longer. And in telling us that the lady realizes, "I have some leverage here." And now she knows what to do! But there's another layer. Because we ask her for permission whether in the future, we can refer anyone else who calls us asking about an attorney to her. "Oh sure," she says, "I'd love that."

"On the other side, there were Princeton students that had never run a venture, did not have a customer base, and they got all the support, they got access to potential investors, and were told, *Don't go with loans.*"

"We need to invest in the resourcefulness and talents of those we consider poor and let them drive their own destiny."

Mauricio Lim Miller

She realized she has more assets in her network than she was aware of, and thus can be of more help to others. Is that why this peer-to-peer approach is more powerful than someone simply handing out a phone number?

Yes, because people respond best to people in their class status. Others in her low-income neighborhood better learn from her how to get an attorney than from us. That's what drives adoption. When you skip the peer-to-peer step, it can be too big of a jump for people. It's not sustainable. What is best is that someone builds up their own social network, expands it step by step, with their peers watching their behavior and eventually adopting it, too. I like to refer at this point to the diffusion of innovation theory: It describes how innovations spread. Someone invents something new, the early adopters copy it, and eventually, demand hits a tipping point and market penetration accelerates. We see this pattern with behavior, too. People copy successful behavior of their peers. In any class. When we support people in their own efforts, help them do it for themselves, that is the only way we've seen that fundamental change can happen.

You've just taken us on a deep dive into the relevance of social capital and peer-to-peer networks. Now, the upper-income strata has networks plus money.

And they are seen as the "makers" of our economy. On the other side, those entrepreneurs living in and around the poverty level are viewed as "takers" from society. Can I tell you about another eye-opening experience I had more recently?

Please!

In 2020, I had the honor to teach at Princeton and became involved as advisor in the Keller Center eLab. There, they encourage Princeton students to be entrepreneurs, come up with projects and ventures. We mentored these students over the summer, and their work culminated in a day where they presented their business plans and PowerPoints to over two hundred people, including investors and really influential people.

One of the student groups wanted to sell English crumpets in the U.S. Interesting. Another group wanted to design clothing for angry young people. Also really interesting! Naturally, the investors in the room encourage the teams, ask questions like "How much is X going to cost?" and so on. And then they give advice. "You need equity. To start this, you don't want loans. You need equity investments, or patient capital, because you're going to have to compete, learn the market, and be competitive with dress designers. Definitely don't take loans. You need different kinds of capital."

What you're alluding to is that loans, or rather, microloans, are often the only type of capital poor people can access.

Exactly! Again, different treatment. Microloans—often at exorbitant interest rates—is all poor people get, with all the risks attached to it. My mother was clear she couldn't take on a loan. "If something goes wrong in the business, you can't go to college," she would tell me. Equity would have been great for her. I told you she wanted to be a dress designer. She would design dresses after working as a clerk, and in the grocery store. She'd come home, do ironing, and then at night she would design and sew dresses for quinceañeras. She was really good at it, and this is how she saved money for my college. She was good at numbers, too, but she loved dress design. Her best friend, Camila, would make Mexican food, put it in a basket, and go to corporate offices to sell. She was a gifted cook and had a customer base because she was talented.

Both Camila and your mother were entrepreneurs.

And both my mom and Camila would have loved to expand their business. But there was no systemic mechanism that would allow them to show their ideas to potential investors and get equity. On the contrary: We discourage informal entrepreneurship and small ventures. They are often considered illegal, and therefore the income has to be hidden.

And on the other side, there were these Princeton students that had never run a venture, did not have a customer base, and they got all the support, got access to potential investors, and they were told, "Don't go with loans." Instead, Princeton has now started an investment fund just for these ventures. The students are considered the future of the economy, so it's clear they need equity. Never mind if the money is lost or not—their entrepreneurship needs to be supported. What a contrast!

Indeed. What lessons do you deduce from this for poverty reduction efforts? Equity for informal businesses? And bringing them onto the official radar?

Yes! Give equity to these businesses! In all these poor neighborhoods, people have talents: They repair each other's houses, they do rich people's driveways. We need to recognize informal entrepreneurship, have investment funds to let them grow, have licensing be available and not discouraged, all of that. Certifications need to be given to them at an early stage and, again, investment capital and recognition.

Instead of the focus on entrepreneurship in poverty reduction that you're proposing, we hear a lot about making waged work pay more. Will a minimum wage help fight poverty?

Well, in some states, it will help. But it's not the silver bullet that's going to get a poor person far ahead. It's the same with universal basic income. It's nice, but not a universal game changer. See, take my mother again—I keep on drawing on her as an example because it's so paradigmatic for poor families. She had jobs. The problem is, they are dead-end jobs. She couldn't improve. She could survive. Even if you get fifteen dollars an hour, depending on where you live, you may survive on that, but you can't save money to get your kids to college.

So you're saying let's not take universal basic income or minimum wage as an excuse to not make structural changes in how we treat people.

Correct! Let's recognize the impact that everyday people's efforts have on their life and community and then give them access to investment and resources commensurate with the impact their efforts can have. That's how we treat ventures of the privileged: one might attract a million in funding, another five hundred thousand. When that nuance is missing, it looks like charity—which is why universal basic income and unconditional cash transfers haven't worked. They still promote our families as charity cases. We need to invest in the resourcefulness and talents of those we consider poor and let them drive their own destiny. They have the capacity embedded within them. As long as we exclude them and treat them differently, we continue to disempower people—overwhelmingly people of color and women.

And it hurts the overall economy! 70 percent of the world's population only has access to 3 percent of the wealth in this world. 3 percent of the wealth! How are you supposed to build assets with almost nothing that's available to you? The poor still build assets. But it's hidden, and far below potential. If we could recognize each other as resources—think how much talent and wealth we would unleash.

Mauricio Lim Miller spoke with Konstanze Frischen.

Mauricio Lim Miller is the founder of the Family Independence Initiative (now UpTogether) and the Community Independence Initiative. Having seen firsthand the faults of the U.S. social services system and anti-poverty approaches, Mauricio was frustrated watching the same families cycle in and out of social service agencies, while the financial resources designed to support them did nothing to build their economic or social mobility. The Community Independence Initiative takes this philosophy global. It is an international collaborative dedicated to self-help initiatives that incorporate principles for establishing a society where mutuality—sharing and working together—is the standard of behavior. What makes Community Independence Initiative's approach different from most current anti-poverty work is that it assumes low-income people are resourceful and capable, and it recognizes and supports efforts by the residents themselves. Community Independence Initiative does not start or lead projects, but once families begin a project and add their own resources and energy, it helps bring funds, recognition, and connection to their efforts.

Beyond Coal

Brandon Dennison

Brandon Dennison's family ties to Appalachia date back to the eighteenth century. A proud local entrepreneur and changemaker, he tells a story of the region that goes beyond the tropes of coal and poverty: of people making informed choices to stay, of creativity and business acumen. And of politicians on the right and left who instead of understanding what is happening at the grassroots resort to ideologically colored instruments that fail to yield results. A conversation about small businesses, local employment, and unlocking pride and purpose.

Brandon, you're from the Appalachian region. Do you find Appalachia represented adequately in the media these days?

No, not at all. By either media on the left or the right. It's typically an extremely oversimplified view. I mean that economically—there's a lot more to Appalachia than coal. Coal has been very dominant, yes, but there's so much more than just that. I mean that politically—yes, Trump has been very popular here, but there are layers to Appalachian politics that you don't see on a red-and-blue map on election night. I even mean it racially—there is more diversity here than people realize. And there's also cultural diversity. Funnily, in recent years, Appalachia has become strangely cool in a hipster sort of way. But the stereotypes and unspoken biases persist. When I tell people where I'm from when I'm traveling, a lot of times they act sorry for me: "Oh, that must be so tough."

So if you were to highlight the essence of Appalachia and her people, what would you say?

There's a lot of authenticity and humility in Appalachia. People don't put on airs. There is a lot of creativity, too. And it's not necessarily the sort of creativity that would land a sleek product on the shelf of a big-box store. What people are good at is taking a little bit of this and a little bit of that and putting it together to make something work.

Appalachians live humbly. Most people tend a garden in their backyard. Many hunt for food and not just because it's fun, but because it fills the freezer up over the winter. Same with fishing. We are in tune with our land.

How does the misunderstanding of Appalachia fall across political lines?

On the left, the thinking is often like, "Well, government programs have put more money into Appalachia than most other regions. Why don't those people vote Democrat when the Democrats are giving them so much?" The answer is that people don't want to have to depend on government subsidies to survive. They do it because they need to feed families, but it doesn't mean they're going to be happy about it. A lot of government programs take away a person's sense of agency and pride in a way that can be quite damaging.

The left overlooks that.

On the right, there's this blind loyalty to the coal industry by supposedly business-minded people. We all know coal is a dying industry—it's a matter of when, not if. So why would anyone go all-in on a dying industry? How is that good for our people or our economy?

Plus: The coal industry is a government-subsidized program. The majority of coal is bought by public utilities or utilities that have been granted a monopoly by the public sector, funded by rate payers that don't have another choice. So it's basically like paying a tax. The way the coal industry gets celebrated as a bastion of private sector success is just not accurate.

When everyone knows the coal industry is in decline, but the public narrative isn't shifting, does that not create a cognitive dissonance that is hard to bear?

It does. And what's difficult is that it often feels like change has been happening to us as opposed to us playing a role and shaping what's next. And on top of that, there aren't enough examples in the official narrative of what a newer, better economy could look like. Appalachians have been told for so long, "You are coal country." And for generations we've believed it. But if we're no longer coal country, then what are we? Our leadership has just not done a good job of answering that question. That's why programs like ours at the grassroots are seeking answers now.

But if your question is "Is Appalachia more resistant to change than other places?" I don't think so. Culturally, the pace of life moves a little bit slower here. But I don't think anyone likes to be put through a massive overhaul that they didn't choose for themselves. I'd be hard-pressed to find a region excited about that.

Hearing you speak, values like identity and agency shine through.

Yes. And these must be baked into economic revitalization models. In our model, Coalfield Development, we are a direct employer, and we employ people in very innovative businesses. We show what a diversified and newer and fairer and better economy can look like. Historic preservation and energy-efficient construction, for example. We helped start the first solar company in the southern part of the state. Reclaiming mine lands to be productive parts of the ecosystem again. Building out local food systems. Printing shirts on 100 percent recycled-content fabrics. And making furniture out of reclaimed wood from dilapidated buildings.

We're creating real jobs, we're paying decent wages for those jobs, and our crew members are part of this. They are becoming pioneers of the new economy and leaders in their community. That builds a person's self-confidence and sense of value, as opposed to just simply being a receiver of some sort of charitable endeavor.

Was there a key experience you had that shaped your view?

As an undergrad, I was a youth director for a Presbyterian church, and we would do service trips to encounter poverty. It ultimately felt like Band-Aids on massive gaping wounds, but it was good for deepening understanding. The last service trip I led was to Mingo County, West Virginia. We were doing home repair for an elderly woman. As we worked, these two young men approached us, tool belts slung over their shoulders, cigarettes hanging out of their lips, shirts off. It was July, it was hot. They asked us if we had work available. I explained we were just volunteers—and they went on their way.

It was a brief interaction. But those two minutes really stayed with me and started to haunt me. They summed up the situation: We have people wanting to work and contribute, but because everything's gotten so messed up and the economy has gotten so distressed, there's nowhere to apply that gumption.

In my view, that's what directly leads to the sense of hopelessness that creates the addiction epidemic. Now, there are corporate practices that inappropriately leverage that despair for profit. But at the end of the day, the demand for opioids to numb the pain connects to this hopelessness: "Things have been bad here, are bad here now, and are going to be bad."

So the question is: How do we overcome that despair? Government programs are necessary but aren't going to transform the economy. Private sector businesses are necessary but aren't patient and flexible enough to address the human trauma that must be overcome.

You said earlier Coalfield is providing jobs in innovative industries. But it's about more than jobs.

That's right. Politicians say "Jobs, jobs, jobs." Now, that's valuable and tangible and important. But the reality is, the job is only the beginning. Humans who have just been through so much abuse, neglect, addiction, homelessness, even lack of safe drinking water—just unbelievable conditions for the United States of America—need jobs but also stability, well-being, and yes, purpose. The typical workforce development system treats workers like plugs to fill holes in the economic system, like chess pieces on a board. And that will always fall short.

What do you do instead?

Whether it's construction or agriculture or solar, we purposely hire people who face barriers to employment. That's part one. And then we're creating conditions where a person can learn and grow and thrive. We employ with what we call the 33-6-3 model. That's how we organize the workweek. Thirty-three hours of paid work each week, six hours of higher education (our crew members are almost always the first in their family to attend college), and three hours of what we call personal development. That's three hours every week to identify barriers, to identify points of pain that need healing and to have reflection and community-building.

Brandon, if you were to formulate principles for policy to apply at large scale—"Here, if you want to revitalize the region, this is what I'd advise"— what would you say?

I would say, "Start with what you have and grow from there." Because so often the focus is on "We need to bring in a large manufacturing plant that can employ five hundred people." The recruited businesses get tax credits and low-interest loans and grants. We "give away the farm," so to speak, for limited results. Not many are convinced to come at all.

Those that do are basically paid to come here. And many of the jobs provided by these large companies are not good-quality jobs. We need to build from the ground up.

Start with the people that are still here now and invest in human beings to reach their full potential. Once we start strengthening our local economies, they will become attractive. We certainly want other people to move here and bring their families and businesses, absolutely. But that will happen more organically.

Second, I'd advise to focus on direct employment. It seems like so many government programs want to do anything and everything except just cover a person's wages. They want to provide technical assistance. They want to provide new access to markets. They want to help with marketing. They want to do infrastructure. But just simply helping start new local businesses and then helping those businesses employ local people who face barriers bureaucratically is a very hard thing to do. And it shouldn't be.

I hate to be overly self-serving, but social enterprises and nonprofits generally are overlooked as an employment strategy. Why not just work through community-based organizations, put people to work on projects that benefit the local community, and create a sense of economic activity in a community that can get the gears of an economy churning again? This, in turn, would then organically attract additional investment.

But then there are those who from an economics perspective might say, "Oh, but in this way, you'll artificially create activities on the ground that are not viable on the market."

But that's been happening all along, just without any trickle-down effect to the ground! When I talk about governments trying to attract large manufacturers, it's not like there's a business meeting and they say, "West Virginia is beautiful. You should come here," and they come. It's like, "Oh, we have this tax credit program. We have this grant program. We have this low-interest loan. Actually, we'll give you the property free, as long as you agree to this PILOT (payment in lieu of taxes) arrangement." That's artificially trying to manufacture conditions and beg for outside investment.

I actually agree our economic development should be more market-based, not less. But is the coal industry a truly market-based industry? No. Is begging a company from outside the region to come relocate here, and subsidizing them to do so, market-based? No. Community-based social entrepreneurs know their markets best. We have to do all we can to support them.

There's this bizarre mismatch with employers saying, "I have open positions and I can't find people to fill them." Yet on the other hand, there's high poverty, high unemployment, and low labor force participation. There are people who need jobs and there are jobs available, and yet they're not getting matched.

It's bizarre. How can that be? The answer is: One, a lot of the jobs that are available pay crap, or the benefits just aren't very good. Two, the jobs tend to be in the more urban areas. It could be a two-hour drive one way for the person who needs the job. But three—and this is my big point, it gets back to the lack of the human-centered focus of the system—the workforce development system is designed by and for the employers, the businesses.

Which means a), it's largely a white, male-dominated system. And b), it's designed with technical needs in place. It is identifying pieces on the board, certain skill sets, that need to be plugged into gaps, which are open positions for these skill sets. It misses the human element, which is the most important element. How are we going to be training this workforce to fill these technical skills when there's no decent transportation, no access to childcare, when there's health issues that people are trying to overcome?

And so my whole theory is that we need to flip the workforce development system to be focused first on helping human beings overcome barriers that are holding them back as human beings. And then from that strength and foundation, work to find meaningful, purposeful employment where it's available, which is where local business creation comes in, to start growing the overall economy.

You're probably hearing a lot of "Well, if the coal industry is dying, why don't you people just move to where there are jobs? And then you don't need to drive two hours one way?"

Oh yes, and it's an insulting way to frame the whole thing because of the deep roots people have that they do not lightheartedly walk away from. But beyond that, people have networks and communities, and without a lot of money, the networks provide at least some support system. But mostly: Moving to where there are jobs means moving to cities, and cities have an affordable-housing crisis. In Appalachia, property has often been passed down through generations, so a lot of folks don't have to pay a mortgage. At least they have naturally occurring, affordable housing. How can they be expected to drop that and go "get a job" they may or may not be able to actually get, in an area where even with the job, they may or may not be able to pay their bills? It's just not a very fair, and not a very logical proposition.

Let's talk about large infrastructure investments, which are a big national topic of conversation right now, including about childcare. How is that conversation landing in West Virginia?

There is overwhelming support, including from our Republican governor and people on the ground in my network, very conservative people: All want an infrastructure bill to pass, and they want it to be as big as possible. It's not the time to think small on infrastructure. If we are going to survive, if we're going to be competitive in a global economy, we can't have people who don't have clean drinking water. Or no internet or even cell-phone service, which has become even more important during the pandemic.

But the how of those investments is critical. We've had big federal money coming to Appalachia before, and local corruption and ineffective state agencies just sort of blow huge chunks of it.

What will be key to avoid this?

During the Obama administration, there was a Partnerships for Opportunity and Workforce and Economic Revitalization initiative. It allowed local community-based organizations to apply directly for funds on innovative projects, including projects that put people straight to work. That can make a difference. The more we can get this money on the ground with trusted community leaders and community-based organizations to allocate it based on their perspective and wisdom, the better. But typically, money goes to the state, and the state has a lot of leeway, and they do what they always do, which is try and build an industrial park to attract a five-hundred-person manufacturer. And then we're stuck in the same cycle.

We've heard you talk about there being pride in coal communities over generations of having powered the country. Is there a conversation around "What if we were the center in America of green energy?"

That's how it needs to be framed. That's how I'm trying to reframe it. A solar company we started is called Solar Holler, which is brilliant because it connects to the hills and hollers of Appalachia, which is a common phrase. And the tagline is "Mine the Sun." I didn't come up with any of this. It's the entrepreneur and founder, Dan. We invested in it and offered the workforce development piece, and now it's exploded to be a fifty-person union company. There is pride behind "Mine the Sun," unlike many of the jobs that are replacing coal, which are service-sector jobs.

The challenge is that the solar industry has not paid nearly as well as the coal industry. It's getting better. Even just in the last two years, we're seeing 20 percent, 30 percent wage hikes in the renewables sector. But part of the resistance to change here is the reality that coal jobs would pay $70,000 or $80,000 a year. No one is going to be happy about losing a job like that for a $40,000-per-year job.

And this is what, not just on the left, but environmental groups in particular, have gotten wrong. But when we talk about climate change policy, extractive communities are thought of as collateral damage. It's like, "Well, we have to shift our economy. That is too bad for these areas. Let's get them some subsidies to help ease the pain." That's sort of been the extent of the thinking.

Whereas I argue: We have the skills and the assets that are needed to rebuild a whole new economy that's more sustainable and climate-change conscious. Let's invest in it. Appalachians love to work with their hands. We love to do the dirty jobs that a lot of folks don't want to do anymore.

Those are fundamentally different messages. "Hey, we're building this new economy and you have to change and go on a government program to survive" versus "Appalachia can lead the way, actually."

And...

And there's a related point in the climate movement that alienates people. This obsession of science with density and urban areas. They tend to look at climate change from a solution perspective that is urban focused. But rural people are not the ones flying on jets all over the world or building steel skyscrapers or mansions along seacoasts.

True! Now that we're on it—what other mistakes are you seeing that might be unintended but are rooted in an urban bias?

Philanthropy has ignored rural areas for too long. Rural areas don't hit the thousands and thousands of numbers that an urban area can hit. So the main philanthropic critique of Appalachia is "Your numbers aren't big enough." But that's been a huge mistake and it's contributed to the political divide. Philanthropy has got to step up in rural America, alongside business investment.

Now, I believe in personal responsibility, so it's not fair to say, "That's a foundation's fault or a government program's fault." That would be a cop-out. But because rural people have been looked down on, scorned, ignored, misunderstood, not even tried to be understood, it has created conditions for extremism to start to take root in some terrifying ways. We are seeing some extremism that is very, very scary.

It is urgent. Back to this infrastructure bill: We've got to figure out a way to tangibly make life better in rural America and in Appalachia. If we don't, some of these really scary trends are just going to keep deepening.

Your family has lived in Appalachia for generations.

Yes, way back. On my mom's side, we go back in Virginia to the 1700s—West Virginia of course used to be part of Virginia. My dad's side, back to the early 1800s. There's a family cemetery in Braxton County, West Virginia, that has seven generations of tombstones where the stories live on. It's up on a knoll under this massive oak tree. I feel a deep sense of connection there.

You have two boys. When you think about their future and their connection to that cemetery...

That's a great question. I want them to have a choice. I want them to not feel pressured to move out, or if they move out, I want them to have the possibility to come back without taking a 60 percent pay cut. I want them to have the choice to be able to do whatever they want.

Brandon Dennison spoke with Konstanze Frischen and Michael Zakaras.

Brandon Dennison is the founder of Coalfield Development. Coalfield Development is creating new social enterprises in a diverse array of sectors in order to model what a more sustainable and diversified economy looks like for Appalachia. It helped start the first solar company in the region, launched out of an old, beat-up ice cream truck. It created a statewide sustainable agriculture cooperative from a former mountaintop removal mine upon which most figured nothing could ever grow again. It employs local workers to revitalize abandoned and dilapidated historic buildings to house new businesses.

These businesses purposefully hire people who face barriers to employment: those in recovery from substance use disorder, people on public assistance, racial minorities, former coal miners. Employees work according to Coalfield's 33-6-3 model. Each week includes thirty-three hours of paid labor, six hours of higher education, and three hours of personal development, thus providing job training and creating new jobs at the same time. This is a tribute to the fact that people can't put their lives on hold to complete an unpaid training program. They have families to feed, bills to pay. 33-6-3 represents a holistic solution to these complex challenges.

Coalfield Development has created more than three hundred new jobs, started over fifty new businesses, and trained more than 1,300 people. It has leveraged more than $30 million in new investment to Appalachian communities.

The Power of Corn, Beans, and Squash

Denisa Livingston

Denisa Livingston is a proud Diné member who quietly rallied her people to pass the first tax on unhealthy food in the United States—part of a broader movement to build a culture of health rooted in traditions and Indigenous wisdom. A conversation about community health, history and how food has been instrumentalized as a tool of oppression—and how planting and cooking can be a means of liberation, nourishment, and joy.

Denisa, what is the nutritional trauma that Indigenous people face?

We are entangled in a food system that is making us sick, and that has been shaped over the last 170 years. But let's start with what it looks like today: Across Diné land, or Navajo Nation, for 330,000 people and more, we only have eleven grocery stores, and the convenience stores sell mainly cheap, processed unhealthy foods. Most often, finding fresh produce and healthy food is challenging. Instead there are chips, sodas, candy—targeted marketing at its best with promotion of *ch'iyáán bizhool*. That means "unhealthy food" in Diné, a term we had to create because unhealthy food was never a part of who we were—but it's a reality now of displays of junk. Take a moment to really imagine this food selection, full of sugar, full of fat, processed foods, week after week, year after year—and the ripple effects for overall health and well-being.

I avoid saying Indigenous nations live in "food deserts," because a desert ecosystem is full of life. I rather use the words "food swamps" and "food apartheid." 99 percent of Navajo Nation live in food apartheid. Almost every Diné family is affected by diabetes, either from a personal battle or we know a loved one who is diabetic. For the first time in our history, our people are dying not from starvation but from "diabesity", a term we came up with that is a combination of "diabetes" and "obesity." And even more concerning, there are heart diseases and liver cirrhosis. Many folks think that's from alcoholism, which is a stereotype. It's coming from the fatty foods. These are all diet-induced illnesses. In the early 1900s, there was perhaps one Diné member who had diabetes.

When looking at this contrast between the past and the present, the dominant narrative tends to blame individual behavior for diabesity, that people make the wrong choices. Why is that not helpful, and also historically wrong?

Traditionally, Indigenous people had a circular economy food system, relying on locally available crops, hunting, fishing, gathering, and harvesting. That is such a contrast with present-day life. And yes, most often, the public narrative tends to blame diabesity on individual behaviors. That ignores the history behind all that, when our Indigenous nations were systematically stripped of their food sources and their food sovereignty. A pivotal moment for our Diné

(Navajo) was when our people were sent on the Long Walk in 1864 by the U.S. government—deported from our ancestral lands and forced to walk to a concentration camp at Bosque Redondo, New Mexico, located hundreds of miles away from Dinétah. We call it Hwéeldi in Diné, meaning "suffering" or "place of suffering." After years of armed attacks by the army, they scorched and robbed our earth, attempting to starve us out, forcing us to surrender. That's where sugar, salt, flour, and canned foods were introduced to our diet, when unhealthy food entered our life. When our ancestors were allowed to leave the camp and go back home, they found their agriculture, their irrigated fields, their livestock, their lifeways, foodways—all had been destroyed. Our food sources were annihilated. All of the plant and animal relatives and all of our fields, land, everything, had been taken, removed, or destroyed. We were settled in a place that was barren and were given food by the government that was again full of fat, and sugar, and flour.

Food was a means of control.

Yes. We can't call ourselves sovereign if we can't feed ourselves. The big issue is that too much big soda, big candy, big chips is feeding us right now, and too few of us have access to quality, healthy, affordable food. We need to take back control of what we eat and revive the culinary traditions and wisdom our ancestors had. With food deliveries during the COVID pandemic, we first received bags of sugar, tons of fatty processed food. We protested against that. Now we are seeing some fresh produce.

When you say "We protested against that," you're referring to the Diné Community Advocacy Alliance, a movement of grassroots-level volunteer advocates that has achieved significant policy changes to systematically change the food systems in Navajo Nation.

Yes, we were the first in the U.S. to pass an unhealthy foods tax, in 2014. It is called the Healthy Diné Nation Act of 2014, and it adds an additional 2 percent sales tax on unhealthy food and drinks—on anything that has no or minimal nutritional value. The proceeds from this tax go to the community to build a public health infrastructure bottom-up, with our community members deciding what to create with it: funds to improve the social or physical environment—for example, hiking trails or Zumba classes. On the last day of December 2020, the Healthy Diné Nation Act was renewed. Earlier, we also passed a sister law, which eliminates sales tax on healthy food, on Indigenous foods, on Diné land.

Changing policy is no small feat; it's an impressive achievement. What are some of the lessons you learned that could be helpful for others to know?

We used many strategies, and ran into many obstacles on the way, including with our own people, and our own Navajo government. One important lesson for us was that language mattered. We had to include community members, we had to include our government in the conversation about food and health. And we had to use the same language, quite literally. Because oftentimes, in public health, professionals use words community members would never use. We talk about health equity, but our words don't reach the ones whose equity we mean. So the question was: How do we turn this public health terminology into everyday words of our community members, so that they're able to react and be a participant in creating change? Sometimes we focus too much on the outcome of strategies and policies. Instead, we need to step back and connect with our people. They have many solutions and answers and frameworks that we have never thought about. In other words, some of the resources, the knowledge, and the wisdom may not come out of textbooks, may not come out of our M.P.H or Ph.D. programs. Instead, it comes from grandma, it comes from grandpa, it comes from our parents.

For example, words such as "junk food" did not really resonate with our community, and it did not resonate with our government either, because in our native language there is no such word, since unhealthy food did not exist in our traditional diets. So we had to create a word for it. That word is *ch'iyáán* bizhool. *Ch'iyáán* means "food," but *bizhool* means "scraps": the unhealthy food, the processed food, prison food, the crap—the C.R.A.P. (Carbonated Refined Artificial Processed) foods—the food that contaminates our bodies, our immune systems, our identity. Using our own Diné language also allowed us to naturally draw this arc to the Long Walk, to the fact that up to this day, we are suffering from that history. We needed to bridge our history with our current efforts.

Another important step was we had to frame the conversation in positive terms, not only about the negative impacts and its consequences—because all that was met with anxiety and also rejection. We shifted to a more positive message, changing what we had originally labeled as the Junk Food Tax to the Healthy Diné Nation Act. Because healthy food is life. In Diné we say, *ch'íyáán yá'át'éhégi dóó tó éí iiná át'é*, and that means healthful food and water is life, it is holy, something that is sacred to us. We had to look at the overall conversation in a balance so that we're not only focused on sugary beverages and fatty foods, but also looking at the big picture, that as Indigenous people, we do have resilience, that we have a tradition of food sovereignty, food traditionalism, that we can reconnect with.

What was key to our eventual success was to frame the debate around food in terms of our cultural identity—that unhealthy foods were beginning to shape who we are, shaping a narrative that we were unhealthy, weak, vulnerable to health epidemics. We had to change that conversation.

You're not just changing the conversation, you're also changing the practice. What are some of the traditional crops coming back to Navajo Nation that you are planting right now?

Oh, I'm delighted to tell you! There are what we call the Three Sisters: corn, beans, and squash. They have been central to Indigenous culinary traditions and agriculture. They are planted together, they are symbiotic, providing each other with nutrients, and providing us with nutrients, too. We have different types of corn—white, yellow, and blue corn—as well as different types of beans and squash. We have traditional types of melons, watermelons, chilis, and edible flowers. Furthermore, we are rematriating some of our traditional crops. Indigenous food advocates have started seed sovereignty projects, and we are cultivating and exchanging seeds between Indigenous nations. For instance, I just received a gift from a friend in Washington, tubers for the Four Corners Diné potato. They are being grown in Washington, but they originally belonged to the Diné people, so they were gifted back to us, and we have planted them here again. At the same time, we're recultivating our ties to the South. Historically, tribal people from the Southwest had trade routes all the way down to Belize in Central America to South America. Now some of our elders are working with other Indigenous tribes there that have held our seeds that they want to give back to us. It's very healing how all of this is being revitalized.

As I'm listening to you...it is all quite emotional!

Yes. It's quite emotional, spiritual work, but it's also very liberating because in the process of doing all of this, it's understanding that food will heal us, and it's about showing us how we recover. This journey is much more fun than talking about processed fatty food. This work of planting, of recultivating, researching—it's about reprogramming the tongue, from all the unhealthy food to wanting to taste the traditional healthy food, to understanding that our ancestors had this rich tradition and culture.

One of the little stories I have that shows you the impact of all of this is from one of our elders who's training young Indigenous people from different parts of the world in land restoration—keep in mind that the food trauma that was inflicted on the Diné has been repeated across the world with other Indigenous people. Now, our elder was training these Indigenous people from Brazil, and they went home and started growing their traditional crops. And when the crops came out, their elders started crying. They were very emotional over what they were seeing. So the youth were afraid, asking, "Why are you crying? Did we do something wrong?" And the elders said, "We haven't seen these crops since we were children." I have so much empathy for that. My own grandma, she just turned ninety, and she is so proud seeing this work and the progress of embracing our traditional food, not just in Diné land, but around Indian country, across the world.

So, you know, planting is an effort of resilience, but also of adaptability, of liberation, of meaningful intentional actions to build back and heal colonization and relocation. We're doing that in the fields, in our gardens. It is joyful! Planting and cooking can be such a meaningful, revolutionary act. We are in a season of reconciliation, reparation, and restoration.

Has this work of yours on food systems been relevant during the pandemic?

Oh, very much so. A lot of what we learned in the process of passing the Healthy Diné Nations Act has been relevant, and also the fact that we have these deep relations of trust within the community that we could leverage during the pandemic.

When the World Health Organization at the beginning of the pandemic said that you have to give power and agency to the community members, I said to myself, "Yes, that's what we've been saying all this time." But then, there was this large gap between rhetoric and practice. The CDC guidelines and what we saw coming from the top down often did not square with the lived reality in our communities. For example, the case of our community member who was the first to pass away from COVID-19. What had happened? He showed symptoms and was told to go isolate, to go quarantine. But where does he live? He lives in remote Navajo. It takes you hours to get to his house by car. He lived where there's no phone connections, no access to water, no access to food. His mother also had COVID-19. When they eventually got hold of them, he had passed away. He died because he was literally following instructions to go isolate—a concept of course that is critically important to disrupt the chain of infection, I do not want to argue against that. But isolating without water and telephone and help nearby?

The guidelines did not land as intended because the officials did not understand the context.

Exactly. In the end, the time of the pandemic has been a moment of building out Indigenous public health protocols and systems that we will be able to use in the future. Again, we had to create the language, we had to translate COVID-19 into our language. *Dikos Ntsaaígíí Náhást'éíts'áadah*—that's how you say "COVID-19" in Diné. We had to translate much more, integrating our collective protection with our language with the community, we had to navigate our traditional ways during the pandemic, uncover its power, that is—especially after the case with the first gentleman who passed away from COVID.

Were you able to draw on history again, as you have done with food?

Absolutely. Also during COVID, we could take lessons from history, to encourage us, to give us strength, and to let us avoid pitfalls. Our elders, our ancestors, had been through hardship before. We went to the archives and looked at what had happened during the Spanish flu, and we saw similarities between what happened then and what is happening now, and that there was not enough public health awareness, that there was no culturally relatable communication.

So part of my advocacy with the Navajo Nation Government right now is to resort to our culture, to go to the archives, to ask our elders, our community— reactivate, re-engage, and recover our ancestral wisdom. How have we isolated, how have we quarantined traditionally? What are those traditional medicines, what did we use? Knowing that will help us adapt in the present, will help us empower our community members, will strengthen our Indigenous public health systems. And again, answers to our questions are not found in textbooks.

Your focus on food has opened up myriad ways to power public health!

It's been quite a journey. Many tears were shed, and many words have been spoken. What we are saying is: We've got to get out into communities. We've got to elevate communities. We've got to bring agency back to the communities. We've got to give people new roles to play in society, or rather: We've got to reinstate those roles, supporting those roles that existed before. We ought to know our ways of collective continuance towards restorative justice, healing frameworks, and community empowerment.

Food has been central to all of this. During the COVID pandemic, the talk that I've been giving is that we cannot just go through the pandemic, we have to *grow* through it. Part of the healing mechanism is that when we literally weed out those weeds in our gardens, and when we seed traditional crops and plants, we grasp with our hands that we have responsibility, and stewardship, origi- nating with our ancestors. Food is a way of connecting with our history, and through that we can discover our ancestors' ways of living, of governing, which were different than we see now. The autonomy, the agency, and traditionally, the power and the decision-making—it happened with the people. Historically, the chiefs called on the women to make the ultimate decision, but we don't see that now. Nowadays, most decisions are being made by men. But when we talk about the past, through our food, it opens up a possibility for us to imagine a different future, where women are fully included and consulted with again.

We are using the hashtags #FoodIsMedicine and #WeAreStillHere. Because with food, we are able to heal our bodies, heal some of the atrocities, the historical trauma, and the nutritional trauma. We need to place emphasis on how we are transforming the palates of our tongues, the food on our plates, and the plants in our soil. And with that, we are able to address history, we are able to address the present, but we are also able to create history for the future. *Ahéhee'*—thank you.

Denisa Livingston spoke with Konstanze Frischen.

Denisa Livingston is the founder of the Diné Community Advocacy Alliance. Composed of grassroots-level community health advocates from various Diné (Navajo) Nation communities and surrounding areas, the alliance raises awareness, informs, educates, and mobilizes community members to combat obesity, diabetes, and other chronic health issues, and to be a voice for the Diné communities. The Diné Community Advocacy Alliance formed in 2012 as a response to high rates of obesity, diabetes, and complications from these health issues among children, youth, families, adults, and elders living in and around the Diné Nation. The alliance is powered by a team of intergenerational committed tribal citizens and community members who volunteer to turn concerns into actions to help Indigenous peoples, focusing on creating momentum for healthy innovative change and maximum positive community outcome.

Defending Each Other

Raj Jayadev

Most Americans facing criminal charges—especially people of color—never have access to strong legal representation. But what if ordinary citizens can help? Tapping into the organizing capacity of communities, Raj Jayadev unlocks the knowledge and wisdom of those with a loved one accused of a crime to shift the outcome of cases. A conversation about chronically overworked public defenders, the imbalance of power in our courts, and the impact of prison—and prison time saved.

Raj, over 90 percent of people faced with a criminal charge take a plea deal—that means they say yes to having committed a crime before their case has been heard in court, before they've had a chance to be found innocent or guilty.

Correct. This is the untold story of mass incarceration. The ugly underpinning reality of why the U.S. incarcerates more people than any other country in the world. The system does not afford everyone a fair trial. Over 90 percent of people will never have their fabled day in court.

How can that be?

What is happening in courts every day is a story that goes more or less like this: Imagine you've been arrested a few days ago for an alleged offense. The average bail amount in California is $50,000, and you can't afford that. So you're going to jail. You cannot go to work, you cannot pick up your kids from school, you're in jail. You are waiting. You don't really know what's happening next. You do not have a private lawyer. You're brought to court for an initial hearing, and there's a defense attorney you are meeting for the first time. They explain that you haven't been convicted of anything, but that you could take this plea deal, and you will go home soon. Or that you could challenge the allegation. That could mean going to trial, of course, and if you do that, you will have to stay in jail pre-trial through the process—which could be months, even years. And of course, you don't know if you're going to win. So you could either take the plea deal now and get whatever time the plea is offering, or you could go to trial, stay locked up 'til that stage, and face what could be an exponentially longer time of incarceration—10 years, 15 years even.

And if you're a person of color, the one thing you do know is that the court system is inherently racist. You know that the juries aren't necessarily going to believe the defense side. You know that the prosecutor is well resourced. You know there have been aggressively high sentences against people in your community. You know that the judge may also have implicit biases against you. So in a situation like that—do you hold on to your innocence? Or do you make a calculated decision?

...a calculated decision where someone's innocence or guilt doesn't seem to be the decisive factor.

That's right. Even if you know you're innocent, it suddenly appears rational to say yes, you committed a crime, and take a plea deal. Even though you'll have a conviction on your record that will affect the rest of your life. Because the alternative looks worse: The trial date could be months later, or maybe years later. And then you may lose. And even on the tail end of that—the way sentence structures work means there could be a mandatory minimum charge for the crime you did not commit. There could be add-ons the prosecutor alleges, like gang membership, that would add extra years to the punishment. All these factors come into play that make it rational to decide not to roll the dice. Actually, there's not much decision-making, because that presumes you have option and freedom to decide. But generally, in cases like this, people feel they do not have agency. They feel coerced into a decision. And their life has already been broken.

But everyone has access to a public defender, right?

Correct. Nine out of ten people faced with a court case in the U.S. will not have the resources to pay for a private attorney. That's 90 percent—and as you say, they'll get a public defender. The public defender is the one legal advocate, the mouthpiece of any sort of attempt to secure freedom. But while the public defender may have all the best motivation to do heroic work, the reality is they are pretty isolated inside the court system, are chronically under-resourced and have piles of cases to work through. They are simply unable to afford a lot of attention to any individual case.

That's why there's a system-inherent incentive for them to offer plea deals?

That's right. It goes full circle. There's a factory approach inside the courts. As many people as possible are processed day by day. The plea deal is an integral part of that system. There's no default infrastructure to support everyone to go to trial. That wouldn't be possible, the system would break down. That's why I would say the value that guides the criminal punishment system in its day-to-day work is not liberty, or freedom. It's efficiency.

Now, you've found a way to inject more resources into the court system to bolster the defense side. Participatory defense is the methodology, and it works at the most abstract level by tearing down the walls that separate the courts from the communities and drawing on the resources and capacities of families and friends of a person facing charges.

Yes, we basically took lessons from community organizing and applied that to the judiciary. Let me step back to explain.

Participatory defense was born out of community organizing. In community organizing, there's that unspoken blueprint of how to deal with police violence locally. When someone gets assaulted, gets injured, maybe even killed by police—a community group rises up, supports the family, takes to the streets, marches, protests, maybe holds the individual police officer accountable. And usually, the blueprint ends after that point. When people came to our organization back in the day and said, "I got court next week," we did not know what to do besides perhaps throw a car wash to try and raise some bail money. What usually happens from the point of view of a community whose loved one has been arrested is that all you can do is just hope and pray and wait for the system to spit them out, at some point, with the least amount of harm. You feel powerless.

And thus, at the beginning, we just saw the court outside of our arena of change. We thought our work is done out in the streets, and the courts are for the lawyers and the judges. What we didn't know then, but self-critique helped us see later, was that we were limiting ourselves based on our own assumptions of what silo community organizing should exist in.

You took organizing out of the streets and into the courts.

Yes. Eventually, we took the exact same tactics and strategies that we used for our organizing work around police violence and applied it to the court system: Which is to say, we got friends and family of a loved one accused of a crime together and collectively tried to road-map a strategy forward. So that the loved one under the gun of the institution, meaning the courts, had support, and that we'd collectively work together to push back, bend back, and maybe beat that institution. That's how it started.

In other words, you'd start tapping into the inherent propensity and energy of close family and friends to influence the outcome of a court case.

Correct. The family of a loved one accused of a crime may not have the resources to get a private attorney and to buy that attorney's time to interview character witnesses and gather evidence. But they have knowledge about their loved one. They can help mount a better defense and bring in the information and evidence to the public defender.

Family and friends become part of the defense team.

Yes, and they are likely going to be key for any defense strategy. They can, for instance, fact-check a fictionalized police report about what's happening in the neighborhood. If there's an allegation, say that the defendant was part of such and such gang—well, the community will know whether that's true, or whether perhaps—and I'm not making that example up—that gang hasn't existed in fifteen years. They may know that the defendant was not at the place of the crime at the alleged hour—because he was with some neighbors across town, and there are witness accounts of that, and perhaps cell-phone records or surveillance videos that show so. They can make a video biography of the person accused, they can bring pictures from private photo albums showing him doing homework with the children, celebrating birthday parties, making breakfast—evidence of being a committed dad. The community has access to information that is at their fingertips, that is almost impossible for an overworked, isolated public defender to get access to. That's why public defenders see value in the partnership with the community.

All that biographical context also shows to the court that the person is part of a larger community that is invested in the defendant's well-being.

That's right. We developed tools like social biography videos—mini documentaries—to tell the fuller story of a person. And the impact can be immense: It shows to the prosecution and judges that the person in front of them is more than a case file. These videos bring a moment of empathy into courtrooms. It dissolves the walls of the court, it brings the judge into the community, so they understand more fully the context of someone's life.

Conversely, with more information, the community can better counter the arguments of the prosecution.

Yes. Here's an example. The key decision during the first court date, the arraignment, is whether the defendant can be released pretrial or detained pretrial. Whether he'll have a high bail, low bail, or no bail. In order to make these calls, the judge must decide two things: Will the defendant come back to make the court appearances? And: Is there some sort of public safety threat? If the family and defender can develop a narrative based on evidence that the defendant has a job, is a devoted parent, an active community member, with an aunt and uncle in town who appear personally for the arraignment pledging to drive the defendant to court...then they are stripping away any excuse the judge has to keep their loved one detained. Then it becomes increasingly impossible for the judge to deny someone their liberty and price them out of freedom. And all the information needed for that comes from the family. And in each stage of the case there'll be those types of intervention points where participatory defense can impact the outcome—perhaps even get the entire case dismissed or get out pretrial. That it such a determinative factor on the pressure to take a plea deal or not.

Participatory defense has spread all over the country. You measure its success in terms of years saved, not served. What is the latest number?

Our last count was 10,208 years of time saved from incarceration. That means years someone is home, can be there for the children, can earn a living. The impact of incarceration on families is not just individual. It's a generational trauma that you see being handed down to the third or fourth generation. And when you think about what one year of being vanished does to a family community, multiplying it by those numbers is mind-boggling. As good as the number is, it warns us what the system has threatened to take away from people. And we'll never know what happens to the young person who is at this pivotal fork-in-the-road moment but ends up going to prison instead of university. We'll never know what would have happened if their parent had come home, how they could have re-guided that young person's life. And so what we've got to do is try to bring folks home so that those stories can exist.

Do you see any promising shifts, especially over the last one to two years?

People have very justifiable reasons to be the most hopeful they've been in

"Even if you know you're innocent, it suddenly appears rational to say yes, you committed a crime, and take a plea deal. Because the alternative looks worse."

"Our last count was 10,208 years of time saved from incarceration. That means years someone is home, can be there for the children, can earn a living."

Raj Jayadev

decades. Because the criminal court system doesn't exist in a vacuum. It is a political social construction, and so it is influenced by what is happening outside of its walls. And everything changed, I think, after the murder of George Floyd, and in the public response. The impact of that, of the public response to the killing, went beyond policing. Policing is just the first point of contact, the entry point. And there is a heightened consciousness now that this violence penetrates the entirety of the system. And so that new political consciousness is going to impact what happens with incarceration.

What are signs for that?

We see shifts that are in some ways perhaps redemptive moments. Take mandatory minimum sentences. It's a completely ridiculous idea: that anyone confronted with a certain charge gets a certain minimum number of years, regardless of the circumstance or situation, with no discretion for individual situations. But now, those mandatory minimums are being challenged. The same is happening with so-called "enhancements" that are by definition racist, like gang enhancements. They only ever impact communities of color. Now we are waking up to that. Drug charges are being seen in new light, too. Whether you look at substance abuse as a health issue or as a punishment issue produces totally different outcomes, and we know these outcomes fall along racial lines. Drug charges have been a tool of control over Black and Brown communities, and now they are being reexamined. Not that the arguments against those measures were never made before. They were. But they are being received by a different political moment, they are seen and understood differently. There's this appetite for us as a nation to take a look in the mirror.

But then there's another factor that has more to do with money than with political awakening.

You're alluding to the costs of maintaining a huge prison population?

Yes. Even for someone who does not see the justice aspect of the points I made, they will likely concede that the infrastructure of incarceration is so exhausting and so depleting that it's decimating jurisdictions in states and counties. In California, where I'm at, there's a multiyear effort under way to depopulate the prisons because they were so severely overpopulated that there were Supreme

Court findings demanding that density and numbers get reduced.

And do these two unrelated schools of thought—the reckoning side and the economic argument—do they come together and reinforce each other?

They do, because what the overpopulation side of the equation forces administrations to do is to reverse engineer the system. And when you reverse engineer the system, you'll start with the question "Well, why do we have so many people in prison? What can we change at the faucet of the courts so that we're not sending so many people in?" And you end up quickly at the point of considering release valves for people that have perhaps unnecessarily long sentences and that clearly are not going to harm anyone. We're talking about elders and seniors that are sentenced to fifty years and more when they were accused of a crime when they were fourteen, fifteen years old. All that practice is being reexamined. And what's really interesting now is to examine what happens, in California at least, when people are coming home from prison.

What is happening?

All those initial presumptions that allowed this type of atrocity in the first place—people that are being sent to prison are inherently dangerous, they are inherently flawed, they will always put the public in jeopardy if released— all these presumptions turn out to be wrong. Because people are home now. And their recidivism rate is less than people that do small jail stints. Very few people go back. Turns out everyone is just trying to live their life.

The same pattern happened during COVID. Across the U.S., counties greatly reduced their jail populations because of the public health crisis. In my county, Santa Clara, we went from five thousand to something hovering around two thousand. Our jail population has not been that low for decades. And again: Crime did not increase, people did not reoffend.

And because these are measurable patterns, they start making the argument to people: "Well, why were they in jail to begin with? Is that really the solution?" When you realize the sky didn't fall, crime rates didn't increase, perhaps it turns out to be a totally false bill that we needed incarceration to begin with.

Well, it is the case that the U.S. stands out in a global context in terms of the rates at which people get incarcerated.

That's right. We have the highest incarceration rate in the world. So that in itself is a sign that there's nothing natural about our system. And we suffer as a result. And that's where my head is at right now…The argument of how harmful the criminal punishment system is is a pretty easy one to make. So: Can we as a society move on from tinkering with the mechanics of this criminal punishment system of ours to thinking what would happen if we did not have this system at all? What if we didn't have the thinking and the thought process that arrived at it, with its roots in slavery, and what would we do in its place? And I think that's really where we're at. And not that I have any sort of ready-to-insert answers, but I think that's where we're at.

And what could the next step be in that thought process?

I'm going to sound super abstract here, and I apologize. But I think it's okay for us to kind of have more questions at this point than anything. So the next step is going to be about questioning what values get satisfied by the criminal punishment system. Right now, core values are vengeance and punishment. And what should or could these be replaced with? And then what do those values construct? And if that value, for example, is safety for all, or rather, safety and well-being for all—which is in some ways, if you have a politicized way of looking, a large tent that people from different walks of life can sit under—then the next question is: What is the society we create that allows for safety and well-being for all? And how do we guard against the vulnerabilities of our society that have jeopardized these values for some people? And I think with that perspective, we're going to look at the structural issues underneath the ground that have created the criminal court system. We are going to look at issues of poverty, disenfranchisement, mental health, abuse, about why people commit harm, what fuels it.

And focus on solving those, rather than on punishment of crimes that might be fueled by these conditions in the first place?

Yes. If we had a different understanding of resource distribution and meeting people's needs, maybe the need for prisons and jails and police isn't inherent. And maybe if we created that world and took steps towards it, our current assumptions about the kind of criminal court system we need aren't as necessary anymore.

Raj Jayadev spoke with Konstanze Frischen.

Raj Jayadev is the co-founder of Silicon Valley De-Bug. Silicon Valley De-Bug is a community organization based in San Jose, California, that uses community organizing to advocate for racial and economic justice. Through their work towards ending mass incarceration, they created "participatory defense"—an organizing model for families and communities who have loved ones entangled in the criminal punishment system to impact the outcome of cases and collectively transform the landscape of power in the courts. After doing work locally for twelve years, Silicon Valley De-Bug now trains communities across the country and coordinates the National Participatory Defense Network—comprised of movement organizations in over thirty cities across the U.S.

A Road to Repair

Danielle Sered

Does incarceration make us safer? Or repair harm? If so, why do a majority of survivors of crime opt for an alternative to prison for the person who hurt them when given the choice? A conversation with Danielle Sered about what breeds violence, the pragmatism of survivors, the transformative power of genuine remorse, and what it takes to build safety for all.

Danielle, you argue—which may sound paradoxical—that incarceration increases violence. How so?

We know from research what contributes to violent behavior. On the structural side, it is factors like poverty and a lack of a robust social-service infrastructure. At an individual level, violence is driven by shame, isolation, exposure to violence, and an inability to meet one's economic needs.

Incarceration exacerbates all of those things. The core features of prisons are shame, isolation, exposure to violence, and the inability to meet one's economic needs. And so we've baked into our responses to violence the exact things that generate it. It's like showing up at a house fire with a hose full of gasoline and acting surprised when the flames rise higher. Prison is not just ineffective at producing safety. Prison is impeccably designed to produce more violence.

But supposedly we're building prisons to help us be safer?

The reason we prioritize incarceration over schools and incarceration over roads and incarceration over a public health infrastructure is because we're told a story about some imagined monstrous "other" from whom we have to be protected at any cost.

We have made the choice to incarcerate people not because of an act of shoplifting or a drug possession. We have chosen incarceration because we have been persuaded that prisons are the only way to protect ourselves and the people we love from grave harm. And we have decided that protection is worth any costs—morally as well as financially.

The underlying narrative that drives our attachment to incarceration is fundamentally a narrative about violence, and it's a narrative that is deeply racialized. It has always been either overtly or implicitly a narrative about Black and, to a different degree, Brown people in America, with lineage to slavery, to convict leasing, to Jim Crow and all the ways that the racial hierarchy in this country has persisted and remained enforced.

It is my belief that if we don't challenge that narrative directly, it will continue to feed every policy decision we ever make. As a nation we have to decide: Who do we believe is harmed? Who do we believe causes harm? What do we believe the people who cause harm owe, and to whom? And what do we know will make us all safe? If we avoid those questions, we'll continue to incarcerate the greatest proportion of our own population of any nation in human history.

And our choices and policies have increased our prison population significantly in your own lifetime, right?

Yes. By my best estimate, on the day I was born, there were 443,850 people locked up in the United States. There are more than 2.3 million today. The story is that more people are locked up because more people have done the things that get people locked up. But what is in fact true is that more people are locked up not because of an increase in harm, but because we have criminalized a greater portion of human behavior, and we have dramatically increased the punishments associated with that criminalization. Those were policy choices that we made and that we could just as easily reverse.

Is a world without prisons possible?

If we want a safe world, it has to be. At Common Justice, we envision a world without violence and then work to make it possible, fully aware that we aren't likely to achieve it in our lifetimes. That work starts with understanding the relationship between prisons and safety and violence. Whether we look to the vast sociological literature or to people's lived experience, any rigorous analysis lands on prisons as being criminogenic, meaning they increase the likelihood of future criminal behavior. So again: We have created a response to violence that generates it.

When I say I want to see an end to prisons, I say so in part because of the brutality of prisons. But centrally, I want to see an end to prisons because I want to see an end to violence—I want to see people safe.

So what is the alternative?

There will have to be countless solutions—not just one, but a dynamic, growing, varied ecosystem of them. One among them, and the one I practice and know best, is restorative justice. Part of what is promising about restorative justice is its emphasis on accountability rather than punishment. We tend to use those terms interchangeably in our culture. And not only are they not synonymous, but increasingly I've come to understand them as antithetical. Punishment is passive. Punishment is something someone does to me. All I have to do to be punished is not escape it.

Accountability is different. It's active. It requires that I acknowledge what I've done. I acknowledge its impact. I express genuine remorse. I make things as right as possible, ideally in a way defined by those who were harmed. And I become someone who will never cause that harm again. Accountability is some of the hardest work any of us will ever do. And unlike punishment, it is actually transformative.

It's transformative for the people who are accountable. Rather than diminish their dignity, it requires that they step into their human dignity, and from that place act as agents of repair of what it is they have broken. It is transformative for communities because it works: People who previously caused harm stop causing harm. And every time that happens, a community becomes safer.

But it's also transformative for survivors. We tend to punish and incarcerate in the name of survivors, but we never actually ask survivors what they want.

What do survivors want?

It's important to remember that fewer than half of survivors call the police in the first place—half—so shame on us for pretending that's a victim-centered system.

At Common Justice, we only take cases if the survivors agree. So we ask people who have sustained serious harm whether they want to see the person who hurt them incarcerated or want them in Common Justice, where we divert violent felonies from the court system into a restorative justice process. 90 percent choose Common Justice. 90 percent! It's a wild number.

Why do you think such an overwhelming majority of survivors opt for restorative justice?

At first I thought people were better than I knew—full of mercy and of generosity and of unending goodwill. And I think some of us are. But that wasn't most of why people said yes: It was something else. I should have known as a survivor myself that survivors are deeply pragmatic. At the end of the day, there are two things we can't stand. We cannot stand the idea of going through it again. And we cannot stand the idea of someone else going through it.

So when survivors are faced with a choice between two options, no matter how much rage we feel, no matter how much fear we feel, no matter how much loss we've sustained, we are going to choose the things that we think can prevent those two things.

And it's not incarceration.

No. The people hardest to persuade that incarceration will deliver on those promises are the people who have lived in neighborhoods where incarceration is most common. They have paid the price of incarceration's failure with their enduring pain.

If incarceration worked to produce safety, the United States would be the safest country in human history. Not only that, but the Black and Brown neighborhoods in which incarceration has been deployed most would be these havens where people had to tell tales about a terrible ancient past before prisons came and made them all safe. That is not the reality.

Survivors understand that incarceration will not change the underlying conditions that made them unsafe in the first place, will not simply turn their neighborhood into a safe one, will not change the specific person who hurt them into someone who won't hurt them again or hurt others, will not deliver them the healing that it promises them.

And to be clear: You are speaking about survivors of crimes of violence, right? Assault, stabbings, armed robberies, attempted murder even?

Yes. It's important to remember that more than half of the people locked up in the United States are locked up for crimes of violence, which means just numerically we can't reduce incarceration by more than half if we exclude a full half of the incarcerated population. Conversations about ending mass incarceration are not genuine if they stop when they turn to violent crimes.

Okay, please continue.

Well, just to bring the point home: We have 2.3 million people in prison and spend billions of dollars that are based in part on an assumption that incarceration heals survivors. And there is no evidence anywhere at all that it does so. The lack of rigor, let alone the immorality of that, is so striking.

And that matters because when we consider new approaches, we often measure those approaches against perfection. But instead we should be asking: "Compared to what?" Incarceration could not be farther from perfection. So even experiments that are hugely flawed, even experiments that get a ton wrong, even experiments that miss the mark in countless ways will still be better. Our future will be built into the lessons of those kinds of experiments.

What makes you optimistic about our future, given the grim reality of mass incarceration?

It is arguably a funny time to be hopeful, but I don't think I've ever been more optimistic about our prospects at ending mass incarceration in our lifetimes than I am nowadays. I believe we can back get to that 443,850 number or better in the next decade. I really do.

Why?

For three reasons. The first is that we've been there before. We talk about reimagining justice and imagining a new world, and I am a deep believer in imagination. But we don't have to imagine a justice system that only incarcerates less than half a million people. We just have to remember the late seventies. We know the number of people in prison is not a product of how much crime or harm is happening—it is a product of the policy decisions we make about what to criminalize and how and to what degree to punish the

"Punishment is passive. Punishment is something someone does to me. All I have to do to be punished is not escape it. Accountability is different. It's active. It requires that I acknowledge what I've done. I acknowledge its impact."

"If incarceration worked to produce safety, the United States would be the safest country in all of human history."

Danielle Sered

people we have found guilty. And so we can just make different decisions.

The second reason is, as I shared, that 90 percent of people given the choice between incarceration and Common Justice choose Common Justice. But when survivors are asked what percentage of people they believe would make the same choice, the answer is almost always 2 percent, 3 percent, 5 percent. Even though they are part of a huge majority. To me this means what we have is fundamentally a narrative problem, not a public opinion problem. It's about the stories we have allowed to rise to the surface and take center stage in our culture about who gets hurt and what they want to feel safe. And it's much easier in a decade to fix a narrative gap than to change public opinion. What you have to do to fix a narrative gap is to systematically elevate those stories, because every time somebody talks and somebody else says "Me too," then somebody else can say "Me too." And eventually that majority becomes visible. To each other and to all of us. And I believe when the majority of survivors who want something better are visible to each other, we will do what majorities do, which is to win.

And the third reason you're optimistic?

A stunning recent FWD.us study found that one in two Americans has had a loved one incarcerated. Not an acquaintance, not a neighbor—a loved one. I have yet to meet anybody who has had a loved one incarcerated who believes that incarceration works. I've yet to meet a correctional officer who believes that incarceration works. There is nothing like proximity to incarceration to persuade you of its fundamental failure to achieve anything of value for anyone at all.

So the sheer scale of mass incarceration has meant that half of us have been close to its horrors. I believe that the scale of mass incarceration actually holds the seed of its demise, because exposure to it reveals its inadequacy and its harmfulness. And most of us now have been exposed.

The proportion of people who know its failings is becoming great enough to drive change. And I think that's part of why we do see a lot of bipartisan support for criminal justice reform, why we do see things moving in states, including conservative states. It's because a consensus is emerging almost everywhere.

And yet, as you say, race is always just beneath the surface.

It is not beneath the surface, it is the thing itself. It is everywhere. And the racialized narrative about Black people committing violence is a huge threat to our prospects of winning. Because that racialized narrative has a history of being a winning narrative if what you want is to be elected. There is nothing else that it wins us. It doesn't win us safety. It doesn't win us justice. But it has for too long won people elections. We have to resolve that disconnect between what is truly an increase in public consensus that mass incarceration has to end and the behavior of our elected officials, who continue to run contrary to that consensus.

But I do think that those of us on the side of reform bear some responsibility for our losses. When we have the truth and the people on our side, and we're still losing, we have to ask ourselves why. And I think some of it is because our ratio of critiquing to offering an affirmative vision is imbalanced. Very often we spend a disproportionate amount of our work talking about what isn't working and not enough of it talking about what we are doing, what we can do, what is possible, what will animate people to transform. I see that beginning to shift, and perhaps that's really the main reason I am so optimistic.

Is part of our resistance to reform simply fear—fear of getting something wrong and then that becomes the only story we hear about, even among the thousand examples of what went right?

I think that's exactly right. Many of us know the infamous Willie Horton story—a man serving a life sentence for murder who participated in a Massachusetts weekend furlough program and committed assault and rape while on furlough. It became a political nightmare, especially for Governor Dukakis when he ran for president, and it was a bracing and lasting lesson for others in office. What we forget is that the furlough program had a 99 percent success rate. That's a pretty extraordinary intervention—but it didn't protect against the politics of the time. One lesson is that we are not fighting a data battle— the data has always been on our side—we are fighting a narrative battle. One part of winning it will be exercising the discipline to ask of any new interventions: "Compared to what?" The media never runs sensational stories about somebody who committed a low-level crime and was incarcerated for a long period and then came home and committed a worse crime, even though that happens all the time. Prisons are off the hook when they fail to produce safety.

Even when the media does report about high recidivism rates for people coming home, the stories are typically leveraged as a reason that we should invest in more prisons and more police, as opposed to saying: "Here was this person who committed a relatively small infraction, then we staged this costly and cruel intervention, and now that person has done something far worse. What the hell is that intervention? Where's the logic model? What are the costs associated with it, financial, human, and otherwise? Where are the outcomes?" That would be a line of inquiry to actually hold prisons and the people who steer people into prisons, including prosecutors, accountable for the outcomes.

Are approaches like restorative justice more common outside the United States?

Yes, more common, and at a larger scale. But remember that these approaches have roots in Indigenous cultures around the world, including on this land. And the approaches are more common here than we realize, too. They are everywhere—in the ways human beings address problems and harms that arise between them when they don't want to engage law enforcement. We tend to overlook the abundance of practices and knowledge and skills that already exist. A future without prisons and without violence is not just some imagined future—it's mostly a future with a great deal more of things we know already.

Including what we know about feeling safe?

We do an exercise that's become common in our movement where we ask people to envision a time they felt safe. And I've done this in rooms of four people and in rooms of four hundred. We ask people to really envision: Where were you? Who were you with? How did it smell? How did it feel? And we ask people to share what they imagined, and people say "In my mother's arms as a kid," they say "At home with my partner and my child," they say "At my neighbor's house that I used to go to when my home wasn't safe," they say

"On my grandmother's porch," they say "On my block," they say "Before the streetlights came on when all the kids were out and playing together."

What no one ever says is "When a police car pulls up." What no one ever says is "As close as possible to the nearest prison."

When we think about our own safety, we think about relationships. And yet when we pose the question collectively, "How do we produce safety?" the answer we hear is armed officers and cages. But the truth is: The things we know from our own experience are the right answers for society, too. We produce safety in relationship with others. To the degree that incarceration—even apart from its other brutalities—is built on separation, it will always run contrary to the sustenance and continuity of relationships, which is what fundamentally creates a safe social fabric.

Danielle Sered spoke with Konstanze Frischen and Michael Zakaras.

Danielle Sered is the founder of Common Justice. Common Justice develops and advances solutions to violence that transform the lives of those harmed and foster racial equity without relying on incarceration.

In New York City, the organization operates the first alternative-to-incarceration and victim-service program in the United States that focuses on violent felonies in the adult courts. Locally and nationally, it leverages the lessons from its direct service to transform the justice system through partnerships, advocacy, and elevating the experience and power of those most impacted.

In Common Justice's own words: "Rigorous and hopeful, we build practical strategies to hold people accountable for harm, break cycles of violence, and secure safety, healing, and justice for survivors and their communities."

The Goal Is Liberation

Laura Emiko Soltis

Undocumented young people have the right to public K-12 education in the U.S.—but not to higher education in all states. Laura Emiko Soltis's university classrooms are exclusively filled with Dreamers and undocumented youth. A conversation about the country's history of exclusion, the outsized personal risk many undocumented young people experience, and why education should lead to freedom for all.

Emiko, is it true that for some of the young undocumented people you work with, they don't discover that they're undocumented until they apply for college—and are told they can't attend?

For some that is true, yes. Of course, undocumented young people are extremely diverse in terms of where they come from, their life experiences, their perspectives on the world. Some of my students have always known they are undocumented. Most do not know who to trust with their story, and most were told by their parents to be wary about sharing it as it could jeopardize their safety and that of their entire family. Some are extremely open about it and have said "I'm undocumented and unafraid" since they were in high school, inspired by other undocumented activists who shared their stories publicly.

But for many, particularly in Georgia, the process of applying for college is often traumatic and dehumanizing. That's because Georgia is one of three states that has an admissions ban barring undocumented students from equal access to public higher education.

What does the ban mean?

Undocumented students in Georgia, including those with Deferred Action for Childhood Arrivals (DACA) are unable to even apply—much less attend—the top public universities in the state, including the University of Georgia, Georgia Tech, and Georgia College. This policy went into effect in 2011, so it has been a decade that undocumented students have experienced modern segregation from our public university system.

High school counselors are often unfamiliar with this policy. Which means in most cases, undocumented young people find out that they're banned from public universities in their home state while sitting at home alone at a computer trying to apply to college.

Isn't the right to education protected by federal law?

Yes, since 1982, following the Supreme Court ruling under *Plyler v. Doe*. This decision protects the right to free K–12 education for all young people, regardless of immigration status, based on the Equal Protection Clause of the Fourteenth Amendment of the U.S. Constitution, which states that no state can deny to any person within its jurisdiction the equal protection of its laws. But the ruling does not extend to public higher education. As a result, laws and policies regarding undocumented student access to public higher education are up to each individual state.

Why the ban? Doesn't it run counter to the universal narrative that if you work hard, if you're a good student, if you put in your time—that you will be rewarded?

One would think, but it's very much a part of a long American tradition of exclusion. It is not at all a coincidence, for example, that the same public universities in Georgia that ban undocumented students today also banned Black students in 1960. In 2016, Freedom University launched a sanctuary campus campaign to urge private universities in Georgia—which are not restricted by the Georgia Board of Regents bans—to set their own admissions and financial aid policies to welcome undocumented students. And it was so effective that it prompted the Georgia legislature to pass the only anti-sanctuary campus bill in the country the following year. The bill threatened to take away the tax-exempt status of any private university that declared itself a sanctuary campus and admitted undocumented students. Ironically, but not surprisingly, this happened exactly one hundred years after a similar 1917 statute in Georgia that threatened to take away the tax-exempt status of any private university that admitted Black students.

So this is very much in line with time-tested strategies of racial subjugation in the United States. However, in our present era, racial discrimination has adapted to accomplish the same goals of exclusion without having to use the language of race. For example, Georgia's bans overwhelmingly discriminate against and exclude Latinx, Asian, and Black people, but they never use racial language explicitly: Instead, they use the idea of criminality—"illegal aliens" and "criminal illegals"—to justify their exclusion.

Today, in states like Georgia, we have re-created a social system in which we have an entire population of young people of color who, with DACA—which provides a temporary work permit, a driver's license, and relief from deportation—can legally drive to their low-wage jobs, but who are banned from higher education and the right to vote. If it sounds familiar, it is because it is a modern variation of Jim Crow, where we accept a group's cheap labor but deny their fundamental human rights.

Humans are hardwired for empathy, and we have a keen sense from early ages about what is fair and what is not. And yet we are punishing people for the decisions their parents made. Regardless of how you feel about those parental decisions, doesn't it require a level of conditioning to look at these kinds of laws and say, "Yeah, that makes sense, that's fair"?

One would hope that there is empathy and compassion for young people. But again, especially when it comes to people of color, there is a dehumanization process that starts at a very young age. Boys like Tamir Rice, who was shot and killed while he was holding a toy gun, are seen as threats. Young girls of color are hypersexualized. We see it with the police presence in schools and the unequal distribution of detentions and expulsions for students of color.

Part of it boils down to this: Students of color are not given the same grace to make mistakes. For undocumented people, a mistake while driving can lead to either police brutality or deportation. We should all be given grace to make mistakes in our lives that don't have life-or-death consequences.

But I do want to push back on this narrative of "bad decisions" that undocumented parents make when they come to the United States with their children. I am not undocumented and I do not speak for undocumented people. But in my experience as an American citizen who works closely with undocumented youth and their families, let me say this: When you talk to many of these parents, you find out quickly it wasn't their "dream" to come to the United States. Most migrated out of desperation resulting from poverty or political violence in their home countries, usually brought on by U.S.-backed free trade policies and military interventions. No one dreams of leaving behind their homes and family and friends they will likely never see again, to go to an unknown country where they have to learn a new language and work in backbreaking jobs like house cleaning, farm labor, construction, and meatpacking plants for low wages and no benefits. They do this because of the profound love they have for their children. Migration is an extraordinary act of courage.

Thank you for that. How can we inject grace and humanity back into the conversation on immigration?

Well, I think many people who have these feelings or fear of immigrants often forget that unless they're indigenous to the Americas or the United States, someone in their family also experienced something similar: One of their ancestors came here from somewhere else. Some of course came of their own free will, and others were forced.

I believe we humanize the conversation at the level of person-to-person dialogues. There is no "them." It is always "us" as human beings.

I try to model honesty and vulnerability about my citizenship and my family's immigration story. At this historical moment, most people are not threatened by me as a petite, light-skinned Asian American woman who introduces herself as a teacher born in the rural Midwest. I share that I am a first-generation American on my mother's side, and that my mother is an immigrant from Japan. In general, I find that most people in the U.S. like to talk about Japan—its food, its culture, and how they want to travel there one day.

I sometimes ask: "Do you know what the first restrictive immigration law was?" It was the Page Act of 1875, and it banned the immigration of Asian women like my mom. People are always shocked. I explain that it was largely a reaction to birthright citizenship and the fact that the U.S. didn't want the children of Asian women born in the United States to be citizens. In other words: people like me.

I explain that the Chinese Exclusion Act soon followed in 1882, and that it set the groundwork for what became our modern immigrant documentation, surveillance, and deportation system. I describe how this exclusion was expanded to the Asiatic Barred Zone Act of 1917—which deemed all Asians as racially ineligible for citizenship, and that this wasn't lifted until 1952, the year before my mom was born. I can usually get people to agree: Thank goodness definitions of citizenship and immigration policies have changed over time. And if they have changed in the past, they can change today.

Sharing this creates space for people to share their family's immigration story. I listen, and then I like to convey what I've learned teaching undocumented students. I share why my students and their families came to the U.S. I share what they like to study and what they want to do when they grow up. And I mention how ironic it is to refer to immigrants from Mexico and Central America—many of whom are descendants of Indigenous people of the Americas—as foreigners.

How do people respond to all that?

When people hear my own story, when they hear the stories of the young people I work with and the circumstances in which they migrated—it often breaks through. People are willing to make exceptions when they hear one story. And what I often say is that if you can make an exception for that story ...well, that's everybody's story. It's much harder to dehumanize an entire group of people once you've put a face to a story or once you've been honest about your own family history.

In addition to being a social entrepreneur and a movement builder, you are a teacher. You've actually taught undocumented students for more than eight years, helping many of them earn full scholarships to private colleges outside of Georgia. That's not a perspective that many have. I'm curious, what are some of the things that you've seen and learned from them that we should all know?

I realize I'm probably one of the only teachers in the United States, if not the planet, whose classrooms are filled with only undocumented students. Freedom University employs a liberatory education model, or what Paulo Freire, the famous Brazilian educator, also called the "pedagogy of the oppressed." A central tenet is that education is not only a pathway to a career and a degree, but that it can also empower people with the skills they need to transform their world. Another fundamental principle is the recognition that teachers are also students, and students are also teachers.

So yes, I've learned a lot. Most importantly, I've learned what it truly means to be a citizen. It's not something I thought that deeply about, honestly, until I started interacting with undocumented people every single day. I became a

"I've learned about the privilege of being able to move freely. Mobility is rarely discussed when we think about undocumented people, but most of my students have literally spent their lives going only from their home to their school or their home to their job."

Laura Emiko Soltis

citizen by the arbitrary location of my birth, and so do most people in the United States. I have learned that this should not be the basis of one's access to school, to health care, to basic human rights or the ability to participate fully in one's community.

I've learned about the privilege of being able to move freely. Mobility is rarely discussed when we think about undocumented people, but most of my students have literally spent their lives going from their home to their school or their home to their job. Many have never traveled outside of Atlanta because of the serious risks of driving. Most have never been in an airplane or have never left the country—they can't leave if they ever hope to come back. So forget about international travel or study abroad. One of the most gut-wrenching things for me as a teacher is seeing my students grapple with feelings of guilt when they are unable to say goodbye to ailing grandparents or family members back in their home countries.

That's heartbreaking.

I've recognized how living in fear has impacted these children and young people, and how that's going to stay with them for the rest of their lives. Just constant daily fear of wondering if they're going to see their parents every night, the daily fear of accidentally saying the wrong thing. This includes when teachers or friends inevitably asked them in high school, "Why aren't you going to college?" or "Why don't you have a driver's license?" For these good, honest kids to have to lie in order to survive, that takes a severe emotional toll. It's an unspoken consequence of growing up undocumented.

But the other thing I've learned is that my students are just normal kids. In many ways they're exceptional in that they've overcome immense obstacles. Many of them are multilingual. Most of them have been co-parents and adults since they were six. But they're also just kids. They laugh. They love Drake and K-pop and Harry Potter. They have the same insecurities and same dreams as every other high school student. And they just want to go to college and keep learning.

It certainly feels as though anti-immigration sentiment has surged and deepened in America over the last decade—your own governor campaigned on gathering up so-called "illegals" in his pickup truck. But as you already referenced, part of your work is to put this all into historical context. And that includes drawing together what might be considered separate struggles, right?

Yes. Often in movement spaces, we think of struggles as separate. We think of racial justice. We think of immigrant rights. We think of LGBTQ rights. We think of the rights of Muslims in this country and Indigenous rights, and they're all in silos. And sometimes it makes sense that they are separated because many of the challenges these groups are facing are fundamentally different. But the silos also make it easier to divide and conquer. Freedom U is unique in that we are committed to building interracial and intergenerational relationships. We embrace our differences as the foundation of our solidarity and that makes it more difficult for others to try and divide us. Georgia's bans against undocumented young people went into effect in 2011, on the fiftieth anniversary of the desegregation of UGA. The same public universities banning undocumented students today banned Black students in the past. And who has always fought these policies? Young people. Charles Black, for example, who helped desegregate Georgia public universities in 1961 and '62, has been my mentor for more than a decade and now serves as the chairman of our board. Charles was also one of Dr. King's eight students in the only class King ever taught at Morehouse College. There's no better source of inspiration to undocumented young people than meeting the young people who fought against the same universities that are now banning them, and won.

And then what's so beautiful to see: when Freedom University students show up and stand in solidarity with others—the LGBTQ community, their Muslim neighbors, with Black Lives Matter, and so many others. They are seeing themselves and their own freedom struggle in the struggle of others.

You describe Freedom University as a modern-day freedom school. Help us understand briefly what freedom schools were in the past.

Freedom University, our name, is important for two reasons. One, it honors the legacy of the southern freedom school tradition, and two, Freedom University has the best school acronym, which is of course FU Georgia. In 1964, the Student Nonviolent Coordinating Committee in Mississippi organized "Freedom Summer" to challenge the status quo of the Jim Crow South. It was mostly known for its voter registration drives, and it was dangerous. Three young organizers were murdered. But the SNCC also established "freedom schools"—spaces where people could learn from one another for the purpose of liberation.

We incorporate a lot of this philosophy of learning into Freedom U. Students choose their classes. It is completely free. We drive them to and from class. We provide them food. We offer free mental health workshops. We pay their SAT fees, college entrance fees, DACA application fees, and provide them laptops and all of their books. We want to eliminate as many of the roadblocks to education as possible so they can be in a space where they learn what they want to learn and ultimately work together to abolish modern segregation and bring about a world they know is possible.

Is it true that when you meet with your undocumented students, you do so in secret?

Yes. It's very clear that there are segments of the population who do not want us to be teaching undocumented students. It is not far removed from the current attempts to ban the teaching of race and America's history of racial brutality in our public schools. I have received death threats and read online comments encouraging shootings at our school. So we never advertise where we meet. My family doesn't even know where I go to work. And we move locations often so that if word accidentally gets out, we'll be ahead of any danger. It's hard enough to run a school without having to constantly set up shop in new places. But we do whatever we have to do to protect this sanctuary of learning.

When it comes to immigration, or DACA, what do the political left and right get wrong?

So much. On the right, the conversation is often framed in terms of the economy and taxes: "These people are here freeloading and not contributing anything." That's just plain wrong. In fact, it's modern-day taxation without representation. The eleven million undocumented people in this country contribute billions of dollars in taxes every year—via payroll taxes, sales taxes, and others. In 2017, undocumented immigrants paid $27 billion in federal taxes alone. In Georgia, they contribute roughly $350 million in state taxes each year to fund the universities they can't attend. So the economic framing of undocumented immigrants as a drain on society is simply not based on facts.

On the left, you might hear them talk a big game, but remember that the Dream Act has failed to get passed for twenty years. Twenty years! It's not an exaggeration to say that millions of undocumented young people have been waiting their entire lives for this meager solution to provide a pathway to citizenship for less than 20 percent of the undocumented population. The undocumented community is too often used as a pawn for political campaigns and then abandoned once folks get elected. Deportation rates are just as high under Democratic administrations. Detention centers are just as full. Both parties are letting undocumented immigrants down. We study the U.S. Constitution in our classrooms, and the last time I checked, it opens with "We the People of the United States," not "We the Citizens."

Is citizenship the end goal?

So much of the focus is on creating a pathway to citizenship. And that is absolutely a necessary policy step. But when you study U.S. history, you recognize that citizenship will not necessarily protect you if you're a person of color. Citizenship isn't protecting Black people from police brutality right now. It didn't protect the 80,000 citizens of Japanese descent who were sent to concentration camps in World War II. It didn't protect Arab American citizens from profiling and detention after 9/11. So no, the goal is not citizenship. It is liberation.

Despite the repeated failure of the Dream Act, despite the setbacks and the rhetoric, what gives you optimism?

Honestly, what gives me hope is hearing my students laugh. My well-being relies so much on daily doses of cheesy, self-deprecating humor and dad jokes. And what gives me the most hope in these dark times are those moments of laughter with my students. In the face of so much hate and discrimination, they are able to laugh. So when I'm driving a big van of undocumented students on their first college visit or their first trip to the beach, and I look back in the mirror and see my students laughing with each other until they cry? I know I'm doing good work. That's what makes all of this worthwhile.

Laura Emiko Soltis spoke with Michael Zakaras.

Laura Emiko Soltis leads Freedom University, an award-winning, modern-day freedom school for undocumented students banned from equal access to public higher education in Georgia. With the aim of "ending modern segregation in higher education" and creating a future where undocumented and documented students can learn in the same classrooms, Freedom University provides tuition-free college preparation classes, college and scholarship application assistance, and social movement leadership training for undocumented students.

You Are Being Watched: Privacy in the Digital Age

Albert Fox Cahn

Being anonymous in a big city—that's a notion of the past. Nowadays, surveillance technology allows law enforcement to track people's activities with a few strokes of a key. Albert Fox Cahn, a lawyer and privacy activist, lays out why many surveillance practices infringe on constitutional rights and why we need more citizen oversight and a recalibration of the social contract.

Albert, you live in New York, which according to latest counts has more than fifteen thousand surveillance cameras in Manhattan, the Bronx, and Brooklyn alone that the police have access to. What does that mean for someone living in the city?

That no one is ever anonymous. Let's say you wake up in the morning and you leave your apartment: You're being traced by facial recognition as soon as you get out of your building. You enter the metro—the same. But it's not just cameras. Your fare payment is tracked by the MTA. You make a call on your phone, and that data is accessible. Every facet of our life—not just our online life, but also our movement in the outside world—leaves a trail that can be traced. You're never walking unmonitored, unable to escape the surveillance crosshairs.

What happens with that data?

The exact use is unknown, which is a big part of the problem. But we have some data points: In New York City alone, twenty-two thousand facial recognition searches were run by law enforcement in the last three years. Overwhelmingly, they were targeted at people of color, whose communities we know are overpoliced. We can only infer from some data points that there's data sharing between the police department, local authorities, and the federal government.

So your right to privacy is constantly being undermined—especially when you're not white.

Yes.

Let me ask a very simple question first: Is this legal?

It should not be. But surveillance technology develops so rapidly that what the police are doing is a) often unknown and b) partly because of that, it hasn't been outlawed, but it c) also hasn't been authorized. They move in a legally gray area. And because there's no transparency, and surveillance technology can be invisible, it is hard for elected officials to understand how these systems are used or whether and what should be banned altogether.

And what happens is that digital surveillance programs also evade court challenge and constitutional review, because so many of those who are subjected to them never know that they've been in the crosshairs. They are given zero indication. All that is totally off our historical norm.

The larger point you're making here is that the rapid pace of evolution of digital technology has evaded civilian and legal control.

Yes, the legal system hasn't kept up. Historically, the American legal landscape was built around a framework where government's power was to be kept in check, but also, implicitly, government's power to monitor the public was seen as scarce. Privacy was protected by the sheer fact that surveillance was so expensive and complicated. Under the Fourth Amendment, particularized evidence is required to justify a search. And for a long time, economics enforced a high level of particularity. Why? Because law enforcement had to choose: Is it worth spending thousands of dollars to install this wiretap? Is it worth hours and hours of overtime to send a rotating surveillance team to track someone's movement? To have officers trying to eavesdrop on your conversations and follow you around? All that costs a huge amount, never mind the opportunity costs. But with digital technologies, the economics have changed. Now the costs incur upfront, but once software and tools are ready, they can be scaled at almost no cost. With new digital technologies, the police are able to track thousands of people at a time. They can use a geo-fence warrant to capture everyone who's at a protest with an active cell phone. No undercover team needed. They can use facial recognition to capture the identity of everyone whose face is uncovered.

Now, some people may say, "I have nothing to hide." What would you say to them?

There's a privilege in being able to ignore the use of tracking. On a more fundamental level, the possibilities of modern surveillance technology throw up questions that go to the core of the U.S. democracy: What does freedom of religion mean if attending a mosque will potentially get you into a database? What does freedom to assemble mean when participating in a protest might get your phone records logged? When the names of everyone at a gathering can be instantly obtained with one court order to Google? Let's assume you have parents who are undocumented. How will your political actions impact your parents' risk of deportation? These questions don't just chill millions for exercising their rights, they go to the core of our Constitution.

As someone who grew up next to the Iron Curtain during the Cold War, I will say that this runs counter to the concept of open society.

Absolutely. These digital surveillance systems become, in some ways, the perfect tool of authoritarianism because of how they economize control and government capture of our activities. In a world with different technologies but the exact same legal protection, you would have vastly different outcomes.

Draw that out a bit more!

Well, you could have a city with let's say two hundred closed-captioned TV cameras, and you could have rules that any officer can look at these cameras at any time. That would have a relatively modest impact on people as long as every camera needs to be reviewed manually on VHS. Imagine, even with fast-forwarding it would take a huge amount of time to review one tape, let alone hundreds. But when there's a computer vision surveillance system on top of the footage, and then there's facial recognition on top of that, then officers have the ability to query the database and track people automatically. They can now with a couple of keystrokes trace and reconstruct a person's movement across the city—for an entire day, week, or month. In other words, by making these systems easy, we are making them easy to abuse, and we're creating a threat that's different in kind, not degree, from that which is posed from analog tracking.

So the problem statement is clear. We have a concentration of power and surveillance in the hands of law enforcement, scaling incentives and opportunities to do so at no marginal costs, and the whole thing is happening in a black box, with the legislation lagging behind. You're working on changing this scenario, by starting with the basis: citizens.

Yes, we need to bring civilian oversight back into the equation. Long before I was a lawyer, I was an activist and organizer, and from that experience I know it is impossible to pursue change unless we are inviting our neighbors to participate, unless we democratize the debate.

How did that play out in New York City?

In New York, we organized a coalition of over one hundred citizen organizations that came together and led the legislative campaign to enact the Public Oversight of Surveillance Technology Act, or for short: POST Act. Many of these organizations had protested surveillance before, but it was never the center of their work; there were so many other priorities, and so it tended to fall to the wayside. The idea of the organization I founded, the Surveillance Technology Oversight Project, was to create a space to make the fight against surveillance and for democracy the focal point, bring resources and unite everyone under that tent, so that we could make everyone's voices louder.

And then in June 2020, after a three-year endeavor, we reached a major milestone when the city council voted to enact the first anti-surveillance law that New York has pushed through since 9/11—and really one of the first times since then that it pushed through legislation against the objections of the NYPD. The POST Act is now requiring the police to disclose every single spy tool, as well as the privacy policy for those tools, and information on how data from those systems is shared with federal officials, including immigration enforcement officials.

It was a big win, but it is an iterative process. We forced the police to come out with the first set of reports that were then open to citizen feedback. Over eight thousand people made comments. It turned out there were a number of things that fell short of what we think the NYPD was required by law to produce. Which means at this stage, we are requesting better policies than the drafts that we received. In parallel, we are using this new information to push for a ban on facial recognition, to push for a ban on police drones, to identify other ways that we can potentially better enforce the law. In other words, now that we have the legal means to analyze NYPD practices, we can go to the courts and litigate and demand these tools to be outlawed when they infringe constitutional rights.

It seems you've laid out a blueprint here to update the law and bring citizen oversight over technology: transparency, community participation, legislation, and litigation, a cadence to recalibrate our social contract in the digital age.

That is the model that we're sharing with other communities across the country. Our goal is to transform New York from one of the worst offenders to an exemplar of privacy protection. And in doing so, we hope to provide a road map plus technical assistance to citizens in other jurisdictions who want to enact similar protections and replicate successes locally. And local is a key word here: In the public awareness, surveillance and spying are still associated with something that is happening at a different level—in Washington, D.C., or in Moscow. But in fact, there's all these threats coming from our own local police department. Right at our doorstep.

So even though the POST Act in itself isn't able to fix the full spectrum of surveillance issues, each time we make progress, even though it's iterative, we not only get the standalone wins, but we're building this metanarrative of reasserting community control. Whether it's in the courtroom, in the streets, or at the ballot box, we show that citizens are agents of change, able to deconstruct the idea that law enforcement can act with impunity and autonomy in deciding how our cities get policed and how our communities get surveilled.

How can litigation help protect privacy?

We are currently involved in two class action lawsuits where I expect very large recoveries. The reason these numbers are so important is that unless you have a large verdict, given the billions we spend on policing, it won't make a blip. People just see small settlements as the cost of doing business. But really having a high verdict, that wakes up city officials, that has the potential to change behavior. We've seen private litigation as an indispensable part of civil rights work for generations. Nowadays, I see many lawyers deeply alarmed because of the need to defend the basic safeguards of civil rights.

That leads me to one aspect we haven't yet discussed: the aspect of public safety. Because often, the debate about privacy is contrasted with a nation's need for protection—whether from a public health scare or from alleged terrorists.

Yes. These debates get framed in a polarized way, as in "Do we want the safety, or do we want the privacy?" And that's completely wrong. Because a lot of these technologies simply don't work, only work poorly, or when they

> "What does freedom of religion mean if attending a mosque will potentially get you into a database?"

> "Spying is associated with Washington, D.C., or Moscow. But in fact, many of these threats are coming from local police departments."

Albert Fox Cahn

do work, exacerbate bias. They do not increase safety. Take, for instance, Shotspotter, a gunshot location software. Which is, in essence, directional microphones connected to an artificial intelligence system meant to detect gunshots in real time and alert law enforcement to where the gunshots were fired from.

They are marketed as an almost magic tool for the police—they can find out instantly when gunshots are fired any place in the city. Except that it turned out that the software gets it wrong a whole lot: It mistakes car backfires and fireworks and a range of other noises for gunshots. Now, what happens is that these sensors do not get deployed in high-income areas with big mansions and nice parks. They get deployed in communities of color and low-income communities. There are these microphones pointed at public housing projects, listening for anything that sounds remotely like a gunshot. And then almost routinely, officers get sent over into these neighborhoods to look for evidence for something that may or may not have been a gunshot in the first place. They can pull up with a SWAT team at your front door. When you look at cases of police violence, like the recent killing of Adam Toledo, the thirteen-year-old Black boy in Chicago, gunshot location software is often a first point of interaction with the police, and it escalates from there. Which brings me to a larger point: Surveillance doesn't just compromise our privacy but furthers violence.

What would some of the principles be that should serve as guidelines for policy decision making, to weigh safety versus privacy?

There are three important aspects. One is efficacy, what we just talked about. Before we're going to spend money, before we're going to invade people's lives, we need to show—with data—that the system actually works in the real world to solve a problem. And that rules out a lot of these systems. Second, is the system biased? Have you had a robust audit of potential gender bias, racial bias, bias on the basis of language proficiency? There are so many different ways that these systems can get it wrong. And then there's the third question: Who's making the decision? Because if it's the police commissioner deciding, they will decide, more often than not, that this system helps, despite bad data or no data at all. That's where we come full circle: This is why community control is so important. If you don't have people at the table from local communities who are able to speak up, if they don't have the information to participate in the debate...then even the most thoughtful framework is going to come up short.

Given the speed of technological evolution—how do you feel about the future?

Just like solutions are evolving, threats are evolving, too. Technology continues to speed up, companies find new ways to monetize data, to track movements and to use artificial intelligence to judge our choices.

We're going to continue to see new technologies that raise profound questions about what our societies look like and how we preserve autonomy, equality, and rule of law for future generations. And with everything we're seeing playing out right now with facial recognition, with AI, we're likely to see even more invasive, even more disturbing products in a couple of years that we haven't even thought of yet. That will bring these whole debates to the surface again.

Therefore, I believe the quest to make technology work for humanity is a defining civil rights campaign for this moment in history. It will be one of the most central fights we have about civil rights and the rule of law.

Are you hopeful that there's opportunity for a broader consensus here, because the infringement of privacy upsets both the left and right?

Yes. When thousands of cell-phone data get captured through a single court order, I've seen both right-wing Republicans, liberals, and socialists denounce it. Because tech tools are so new, they haven't been put through the political prism yet and become completely polarized. So there is indeed more flexibility for consensus, and that's what gives me hope.

Albert Fox Cahn spoke with Konstanze Frischen.

Albert Fox Cahn is the founder of S.T.O.P. The Surveillance Technology Oversight Project (S.T.O.P.) is a nonprofit advocacy organization and legal services provider. Since 2019, S.T.O.P. has litigated and advocated for privacy, highlighting the discriminatory impact of surveillance on Muslim Americans, immigrants, the LGBTQ+ community, Indigenous peoples, and communities of color, particularly the unique trauma of anti-Black policing. S.T.O.P. works to ensure that technological advancements don't come at the expense of age-old rights. The organization aims to transform New York City and State into models for the rest of the United States of how to harness novel technologies without adversely impacting marginalized communities. S.T.O.P. also believes that directly impacted communities are best equipped to lead this fight and that their voices should be at the forefront for this and any movement. In their own words: "We believe in pushing for radical changes where possible and incremental gains where necessary. We support interim measures, including increased government transparency and accountability, when pursued with the aim of abolishing systems of mass surveillance."

It's My Life

Sixto Cancel

The example of foster care shows what can go wrong in the welfare system when paperwork and bureaucracy dominate children's lives—and what opportunities open up when young people are trusted to be drivers of their own destiny. A conversation with Sixto Cancel, who grew up in foster care, about replacing micromanagement with autonomy, and how we can improve policies and save taxpayer dollars if we enlist the help of those closest to the problem.

Sixto, you've spent the last decade working to update the foster care system. What was its original purpose—why was it set up?

Foster care was designed to keep young children—toddlers really—safe and protected from harm. It's supposed to be a temporary situation that children go into because they are experiencing some type of abuse or severe neglect, and now the state needs to intervene to make sure they have the possibility of a quality life. But the reality is that only 22 percent of people who enter foster care find a permanent home or guardianship. The rest stay in the system for their whole childhood and early adulthood. So, in my case, I entered the system just before my first birthday and was in foster care until I went to college.

So it's not working as intended.

Correct. Some foster care arrangements are healthy, but for many young people, you're living in what feels like a roommate situation, at best. You're not part of an actual family unit. Even if there's no overt abuse, it might be that nobody teaches you how to cook, how to do laundry. But the bigger issue is that the system is not designed to create belonging or develop young people as full human beings, with agency to make choices about their future. That's the fundamental problem.

How did this play out for you?

Well, I think back to my teenage years—it's supposed to be a time where you're developing your identity, where you're developing certain skill sets and mindsets so you can build the foundation for your adult life. I developed these things in spite of the system, not because of it. Foster care splits the responsibility of what traditional parents would be doing among several paid professionals—a judge, a social worker, a therapist, an education advocate, a workforce employment specialist. These caseworkers decide many things: when you learn to drive, whether you can spend the night at a friend's house, whether you can go to therapy, whether you can travel with a school club. It's a huge bureaucracy; there are checklists, and paperwork and sign-offs are needed for everything. There's no spontaneity.

In other words, your life is managed rather than lived?

Yes, tightly managed. My entire childhood was filled with "No, you can't," "It's not possible, wait your turn!," "The system won't allow that," "You really shouldn't," "Stay in your place, you think you know better but you don't." I couldn't attend my beloved brother's funeral in another state because the paperwork was not processed in time.

What?

Yes. Here's the point: What happens is that a young person's development is disrupted. At the same time, that child has probably experienced some kind of trauma before coming into care, and then while in care is experiencing more system-induced trauma. I certainly did; most of us do. You're not taught how to heal those things, so now you're in a cycle where you're trying to set the foundation of your life, but you're also not healing from the stuff you've been through.

You transitioned out of foster care at age twenty-three. How does this "aging out" process work?

If you don't go back to your birth parents—called reunification—or get adopted, or have some type of transfer of legal guardianship, then you eventually "age out" of foster care. For many people that happens at age eighteen, although more and more states are going to twenty-one or up. I aged out at twenty-three, so I was able to go from being a high school senior to moving to college. Then from age nineteen to twenty-three, the state of Connecticut provided me with a stipend, plus some tuition money. So I was able to get that support. But this isn't typical, and only 3 percent of people in foster care even get a four-year college degree. Most struggle substantially with this transition. One in five experience homelessness the day they age out. Why? Because think of it: We're asking teenagers to go from having all these case managers in charge of all aspects of their life, from being micromanaged, to being full-on responsible for their own survival, their food, shelter, job. With zero support. And literally overnight. We don't have that kind of expectation of most eighteen-year-olds, right?

Right! How do people manage?

For most, not well. By age twenty-six, 81 percent of males will experience an arrest. These are mainly related to offenses like trespassing, sleeping in public when you're not supposed to sleep, things of that nature. Half will not have a job or income, the other half will be earning $12,000 per year, on average. So we see a lot of human cost, lost potential, lost futures. There is also a cost to society: negative outcomes of the young people who age out of foster care—23,000 people every year—end up costing $7.6 billion in downstream costs. The system is fundamentally broken.

You looked at all this in your midtwenties and thought, "We can do better." Where did you start?

We started with "The case management process is broken." It's a process with faulty and damaging assumptions. It begins with an assessment of every child, an analysis of risk, a tally of what's basically broken about you and your situation. Then someone generates a kind of life plan for you, with little to zero input from you. And it's your life! Then everything shifts to compliance, and based on how things go, you either transition out of that plan and into a new one, or you're deemed noncompliant.

So we wanted to build into the process a way for every young foster person to say, "Here's what I want to happen in my life. Here are some of my personal goals. Here are my dreams for myself." In other words, we wanted to integrate personal voice and choice.

In 2013, we made a commitment to really work on this long-term. We started a website that allowed young people to learn more about aging out, share experiences, and build the muscle of planning ahead for their futures. This was the beginning of our organization, Think of Us.

You've continued to integrate technology into solutions. Where does it help, and what are its limits that more people should know about?

We've learned that designing for human connection is more important than designing for short-term efficiency. For example, a problem might seem to

"My entire childhood was filled with: *No, you can't*, *It's not possible, wait your turn!*, *The system won't allow that.*"

"With every new policy, let's check: How many people with lived experience informed this agenda? How many validated this policy direction?"

"Someone generates a life plan for you, with little to zero input from you—even though it's your life!"

Sixto Cancel

be: a young person needs to get a job, so they need to build a résumé. The quickest thing to do is just open a Google doc, type together, get it done, right? But it turns out, that's not the intervention our young people need. What they need is someone showing up for them, someone who is not paid taking a sincere interest in their future. That human-to-human element is more important than the completed résumé, which might get done, sure, but the healing doesn't happen, and unhealed trauma is the thing that becomes the biggest barrier.

So these kinds of experiences led us to ask smarter questions the next time. For example, we've since created an online platform that helps young people set up their own "personal advisory boards" to help them navigate aging out. They can invite committed social workers, plus people who have successfully aged out of care, and other adults they trust. The most efficient thing to do is build this with full transparency so everyone can see everyone else's comments within a group. But it turns out that young people's biggest worry is around having the paid professionals and the other adults in their lives who are not getting paid on the same platform. So we needed to develop a new practice model for this.

Asking young people in foster care for input became so important in the pandemic. Can you walk us through how you and your community responded?

Yes, we wanted to build proximity to the federal and state governments, to inform government action on how to best support foster children. The Obama administration had used a more federal approach when responding to crises, but the Trump administration put the child welfare system more in the hands of the states.

Within thirty days, we stood up a website called the Child Welfare Command Center that solicited the input of foster youth. Through the effort we provided an opportunity for young people to apply for a potential cash grant up to $1,000. We had 27,000 current and former foster youth respond. Now, there are 880,000 young people currently in foster care, so 27,000 out of the 880,000 is a pretty good sample. We used that data and passed it on to the feds and to each state, and they in turn used that information to inform what their pandemic relief program would be for young people.

We asked our young people open questions like: "What do you need money for?" I know it sounds crazy basic, but there are a lot of assumptions in child welfare what people need money for, without ever asking them. So we did ask. What besides money do they need? We also asked things like, "What were you doing pre-COVID in terms of education, and where are you today?" We did that for employment, we did that for housing, etc. Bureaucrats were very concerned about college students, but when we collected the data, young people who were in vocational training turned out to be one of the most significantly impacted groups of people. The question is, well, why is that? Do we not value vocational training in the same way? Or is it just an invisible problem? In any case, we can use the data and show, "Look, you're missing this whole group of people who are actually the most impacted, and therefore there should be more investments on this end."

The data also allowed us to substantiate "no" in some cases, and avoid wasting time and money. For example, one state asked us, "Can you do a food security program for college students?" We checked our data and realized this was not among the most needed things for this subgroup in that particular state. Might sound great, it's sexy, and we could easily raise funds, but it's not what young people told us they need.

After Congress passed COVID relief funds in December 2020, did your role evolve?

Yes, and it's still changing, because the problem is changing. In January, we started meeting weekly with the White House as part of their youth stakeholder group, with the Office of Public Engagement. We have lifted up an update from our community of young people every single week since. The first thing we pushed for was a new appointment at the Children's Bureau under Health and Human Services who could help us issue guidance to the states on how to spend the COVID relief funds. Why was this needed? Because we kept hearing from our network of foster youth that although states could tap into the budget, they would not spend it without federal guidance, because they were afraid that they would have to pay it back, that somebody would lose their job, somebody would be in trouble. So that was battle number one.

Following that appointment, we realized that the new problem was that the states couldn't find the young people in order to give them stimulus checks. They couldn't locate them, no mailing addresses. So we launched an outreach campaign to gather the contact information and tell young people that, "Hey, you qualify. Here's what you qualify for, and let us share your contact information with the state." So the idea here is that because young people trust us, we will collect the names and addresses and share them with the states and the states will verify the addresses and send the checks. This campaign is ongoing and showing results. We're fortunate to have a culture and mindset on our team that allows us to move with the problem, because this is a very dynamic situation.

What opportunity does the pandemic create—for child welfare, even beyond?

So, I always think about the six conditions that hold problems in place: mental models, prior dynamics, connections, resource flows, policy, and practice. It's safe to say the pandemic disrupted the conditions holding the current problem in place. There's new money flowing, deregulation, new regulation, which resulted in new practice, new power dynamics. I mean, how many of us responded this year with some version of, "Wow, I didn't know the government could shut down the economy. I didn't know it could tell me to wear a mask, cut my pay to 25 percent, etc." At the same time, we're seeing a collective realization, especially among young people, that parts of our government aren't as responsive as they need to be. They basically don't work well in a dynamic crisis. And more complex crises are likely coming. So now I'm seeing this culture of questioning emerging that stems from the sense that, "Oh, those policy decisions, they're questionable."

So how do we use this transformational moment to really upgrade our government, our policy-making engine to support young people? And that's where there's a nuance and a dance because to swing too much one way or the other is not going to be helpful in actually creating new conditions.

How can we upgrade? How might a future government work better?

With every new policy, let's check: How many people with lived experience informed this agenda? How many validated this policy direction? Like in the tech world, a venture capital investor will always ask you, "How many users have you talked to?" There's more rigor in the VC world about how many people did you talk to than there is from Congress! Also, we now have the chance to connect new policy directions with more qualitative and quantitative research. Here again, let's be sure to ask: How many lived-experience folks were involved in getting the data, developing the right survey questions, interpreting the responses? The good news is that with the right trusted individuals or credible messengers—groups like ours—getting better input doesn't have to slow things down. On the contrary, it can speed things up, by a lot. Just looking at foster care, there's no reason, with the evidence, inputs, and analysis that we have now, that we shouldn't be doubling and tripling down on things that we know work.

Sixto Cancel spoke with Amy Clark.

Sixto Cancel is the founder of Think of Us. Think of Us operates as a research and development lab for child welfare. The organization takes on strategic—and opportunistic—projects with the goal of causing "good trouble" and, ultimately, driving concrete, structural changes in policy, practice, resource flows, power dynamics, relationships, and mental models. Think of Us's ultimate goal is to integrate lived experience at every level, ensuring everyone touched by the system has the conditions they need to heal, develop, and thrive. To achieve this, Think of Us works across the ecosystem of current and former foster youth, child welfare workers, philanthropists, and policy makers to systematically center lived experience.

A New Social Fabric

Sarah Hemminger

How is it that a small organization achieves staggering results of high school and college graduation rates among students in Baltimore? Sarah Hemminger argues that a key determinant of success in life is being surrounded by people who never give up on you. A conversation about showing up, commitment, and the necessity of changing our vantage point and learning from people with different lived experiences.

Sarah, your work focuses on building deep, durable relationships between high school students, volunteers, and the business community in Baltimore to end social isolation. What does it mean to live in social isolation?

It means not fully belonging. It means a lack of relationships that nurture you through life. It is the experience of being treated as disposable, of not feeling valued, of not feeling seen. It goes to the heart of the human experience.

Your lived experience includes a stretch in your life where you experienced the feeling of not belonging.

I grew up in a very religious family. We'd go to church multiple times a week for very long periods of time. Our church community was our extended family, and many of my actual relatives—aunts, uncles, cousins—attended as well. But when my dad found out and revealed that there were financial irregularities at the church, including misuse of funds, the church members decided they would essentially shun our family instead of firing the pastor or changing the leadership. And for about eight years, until I was sixteen, I was part of a place without really belonging to it. I had this incredible love and respect from my nuclear family at home—my parents were caring and close and they solicited and integrated my opinions into their decision-making since the time I can remember. But in the church, no one would speak to me. It was as if I didn't exist. That included not just general members of the congregation, but my cousins and my aunts and uncles. I remember when I was ten years old, the pastor stood up at the end of the service and said, "We're going to take all the kids who want to go ice skating after church today, with the exception of Sarah."

How did you cope?

My parents were very intentional about teaching me coping strategies like exercise and prayer. So I had both this incredibly loving, beautiful childhood experience that my parents created for me, and then this other experience where I understood what it was to be really ostracized and dismissed in a very intentional way. All that has shaped me and my outlook on the world. But what is incredibly important to understand is that my trauma—this isolation—had a beginning and an end. When my family finally left the church after eight years, we didn't walk out alone. Other people joined us. By contrast, for the young people I've come to work with, their trauma and isolation results from systemic racism and has no end—it is their reality 24/7, 365 days a year. Even when I try to wrap my mind around how that must feel, it's just incomprehensible given my lived experience. Just incomprehensible.

The young people you collaborate with in Thread are high school students—in ninth grade when they start—and many experience homelessness, poverty, and other challenges outside the classroom. They rank lowest in their grade. But you don't call your Thread students "at-risk." Instead you focus on their strengths.

Because our young people are brilliant and capable and beautiful. It's the barriers they encounter that make it challenging for them. But there is a dominant narrative that tells them they are at-risk, marginalized, and incapable, which distorts society's view and prevents people from seeing our young people as the beautiful individuals that they are.

When I was in high school, I had a close friend whose mom became unable to work following a car accident. She lost her job and they lost their home. They had to move into public housing, and the mom became addicted to painkillers and ultimately started dealing drugs as my friend was transitioning to high school. His life as he knew it had fallen apart. He failed his classes, he missed more than thirty days of school. But there was a group of teachers who saw him as a human being. They banded together, organized to drive him to school in the morning, made sure he had food, a place to do his laundry, tutoring. They cared for him. He mattered to them. And he became a straight-A student. This person is now my husband.

And then one day, many years later, when I was a graduate student at Johns Hopkins in Baltimore, I was driving past a public high school in an area that has endured years of systemic inequities. And it just struck me that there were young people in that school that were like my husband—brilliant, beautiful, capable—and they might have things happening in their lives that make it challenging for them to focus on their academics. And that led us to asking the principal at that school whether we could build community with these young people. That is how Thread started.

Unfortunately, there is a fundamental difference between the young people at Thread and my husband. My husband had to go through incredible trauma in his youth, but once he was through that he walked into a world that was meant for him and built for him. Young Black men who have grown up in neighborhoods like East Baltimore are not similarly welcomed into the professional world, even if they come with the same credentials. The structural barriers don't disappear just because they've reached those milestones.

How do you manage to break through this social isolation?

When our young people join Thread, we commit to them for ten years—the remainder of high school and six years thereafter. And during that time, we're building diverse, loving, durable, committed relationships with them and around them. We call it "doing life together." Each Thread student has a Thread Family, a group of up to four volunteers. I am saying "family" because they engage in the same way as if the student was their brother or niece or cousin. They help remove obstacles. That might include bringing breakfast so the student doesn't go hungry to school, or giving them rides to school because that's easier than taking two or three buses that take two hours.

What we're really looking for during this time is to show the young people that they are loved, that they are seen, that they matter. And we create conditions for them to find their purpose. That intersection of what they're great at, and what they're passionate about, and what the world needs. That's why we also have programmed spaces like camping, after-school academic support, and community service where volunteers and students get together. Finally, we weave collaborators into this new social fabric. There are enormous barriers in place, enormous segregation, so we need broader networks that can help overcome these. A collaborator could be an employer or an expert that can provide insight into how to navigate systems like legal, health, or housing and can support our young people and volunteers.

As I'm telling you this it sounds so basic, but it's hard to communicate the real depth. Even if I could communicate our community perfectly, it's messy, and so if you're trying to engage someone, whether it's a young person or a potential volunteer or a collaborator, it is almost like saying, "Hey, do you want to join something really messy where you're going to be challenged all the time, and it's going to be super uncomfortable, but it'll be life-changing for everyone involved?"

Perhaps it's this messiness that matters, this willingness to do life together? The data you collect shows an enormous success rate.

Our goal is to enroll 7 percent of every freshman class across the school district each year. We currently work with 655 young people and alumni, as well as over 2,000 volunteers and collaborators. What we've seen over the last seventeen years across Baltimore City Public Schools is that of the young people that have GPAs of less than 1.0 during their freshman year, only 6 percent graduate in four years. In Thread, the average incoming GPA of our students is 0.79 on a 4.00 scale. And our graduation rate is more than ten times higher. 65 percent graduate in four years, and within six years, 79 percent of our students earn a high school degree. And after finishing high school, 62 percent of our young people have completed a four- or two-year degree or certification. And 100 percent remain enrolled in Thread throughout the ten years. And at the core of that success are the threads that we weave together. The lives that we weave together.

These are results that many other programs only dream about reaching.

We are very intentional about our approach. We're not trying to save anybody; we're not trying to make decisions for anybody. We're all in this together, setting goals that align with personally defined success. We don't always get it right. We've made lots of mistakes, but we try to be transparent and fail forward rather than giving up. At the beginning, for instance, we called our volunteers "mentors." We abandoned that, because it presupposed that there's a hierarchy or a one-way flow of help between a volunteer and a Thread student. Wrong. What's required is a shift in orientation and in mindset. We want to flip the "I am here to help you" to "I am here because I need you."

Expand on that.

When we shift our orientation, when we realize we need our young people as much as they need us, we're not just acknowledging their humanity. That's important, but it's more. We start to understand that we're all inextricably linked. That they impact us, not just the other way around.

Here's an example. A young person might join Thread, and the volunteers go in the morning to pick him up and give him a ride to school—but he won't answer. He won't come out. This can go on for months. Now, whose responsibility is it initially to demonstrate sincerity and reliability? We believe that's the responsibility of the adult. Trust takes time. So the volunteers will continue to show up every morning, and their calls might not be answered, again and again. During that time, there's all kinds of emotions they go through. They might feel rejected, they might feel defensive. They are affected by the behavior of the young person. So part of the learning that occurs for these adults is an increase in their own self-awareness. Why am I reacting this way? Why am I feeling like this? That is self-exploration, self-learning. Every volunteer in Thread has a coach whose sole job it is to coach volunteers through this journey.

And then, at some point, the student is ready and will answer the door. I could give you zillions of examples, but here's one, where a group of volunteers were trying to reach a young person for almost a year—a year! And then, suddenly, the young person calls. And when they called, it happened to be Halloween, so they called their volunteer and said, "Hey, I was thinking... you might want to come to a haunted house with me."

And so the volunteer joined them. And suddenly, it was clear that all of those months of going to the young person's house every morning had mattered. It had demonstrated to the student that they cared, that their motivation was sincere, that they were reliable. The frustrations the volunteers might have shown signaled to the student that they mattered. And then they were ready. Their way of opening up and plugging in was the haunted house. And this pattern we see happening over and over again.

That's what we want the Thread experience to be: We want for all people, but especially our young people, to break out of isolation, to be able to exist in community, in relationships where they feel a deep sense of being known and understood and loved, and that they belong. Because equity goes beyond the systems level. Equity also must exist at the individual and interpersonal levels.

Breaking out of isolation, building durable relationships, making a commitment for ten years—your work seems to live on a different plane from the bulk of intervention programs and from the urgency inside philanthropy to see results right away, sometimes with a silver bullet solution. Instead of creating a program, you are re-creating a family.

Yes. Building deep and permanent relationships that will allow students access to resources. To networks that help remove barriers along the way as life happens—I think it is natural that occurs across longer time horizons. This is much more foundational than programs and interventions. It's not even just about graduation and getting into college. This is about changing the way we do life together.

This makes me reflect on a young person in Thread who got very upset with me and stopped speaking to me, and I had no idea why. Eventually—and it took years—he was finally ready and reached out to talk. And at that moment, he explained what had upset him about my behavior and the expectations I had placed on him. We worked through it. And I changed. I learned. And now he has been on staff for four years. It came full circle, but it took time, and in between there are mistakes I make, we all make, and we have to acknowledge them and repair when damage has been done.

If I pushed you to try to get even more to the core of it—what do you think makes it so hard for many people and programs and institutions to connect with young people in a deep and meaningful way?

Let me reflect.

Perhaps I can best give you an analogy. When I was eight years old, I was kidnapped from my bedroom through an open window.

What??

We had no air-conditioning, so we would leave the windows open in summer. I am one of the few children who made it home alive. And when he let me go the same night he took me, I was barefoot in my nightgown and I had to try and find my way home, which I eventually did, and I walked in the front door that was now unlocked, because he had come through the window and gone out through the front door with me. And so I walked through the front door and into my parents' bedroom and I said, "I've been kidnapped." Now, I have a deep relationship with my mom and dad, but understandably, they woke up and thought I had had a nightmare. So they told me, "No, you haven't, go back to sleep, you just had a bad dream." And I said, "No, that's not what happened, I was kidnapped." And eventually, I got hysterical because they would not hear me, and so to calm me down, they took me into the living room and my dad sat me down on the couch. And as you would with a small child, he got down on the floor so that he could get eye to eye with me. And at that point, my dad noticed that the bottoms of my feet were completely black and dirty—because I had been walking barefooted throughout the night on dirty sidewalks. And he just started weeping. It's hard for me as a daughter and also as a parent now to talk about this—because it's a hard enough realization of what just happened to a child, but it's an entirely different thing to have not heard the child, in that moment.

So, to come back to the question of connecting deeply: Even in these situations where you might have the best of intentions—unless you change your vantage point and get on the floor so that you can actually see the bottoms of someone's feet, you're just going to keep talking past one another. And whose responsibility is it to change their vantage point?

In my example, it's the parents because they are the person in the position of power and authority and most privilege. At Thread, we are pushing past the point of "I can't hear you, I can't hear you" to "Okay, I see it. I've got it." Through relationships and trust. That's what we see happen in Thread every day: People of different races, religions, political views, they have conversations and experiences together, and all of a sudden they realize, "I just needed to get on the floor, and now I get it."

And when I say I "get it," I don't mean they'll ever fully get it. As in, you weren't the one kidnapped. But now you can understand it a little bit better, by seeing and acknowledging someone's lived experience. And that's where it starts.

That is powerful. Building on what you just said—when you finally see the bottom of the feet—from that vantage point, behavior you might have deemed as irrational or irresponsible suddenly makes sense.

Correct. What happens when you change your vantage point is you get new data points. You see new evidence. You see the dirt on the bottom of someone's feet. And that new data informs your decision-making. So when you have relationships with people who have different lived experiences from your own, it helps you become aware of how your lived experience has shaped your bias and those new data points then begin to influence your future decisions.

That is why Thread believes it is critical for everyone to be on a journey of growth; our young people, volunteers, collaborators, staff and Board members. Sustained change requires us to understand our own knowledge, attitudes and beliefs, and learn to bridge and bond across lines of difference. Why? Because it is individuals who control institutions, make up communities, and write policies that have the potential to create a more just world.

Sarah Hemminger spoke with Konstanze Frischen and Michael Zakaras.

Sarah Hemminger is the founder of Thread. Thread is a Baltimore-based nonprofit that builds a web of relationships to end social isolation, erode structures of oppression, and improve education, economic, and health outcomes. Thread enrolls students academically performing in the bottom 25 percent of their ninth-grade class. Each student is matched with up to four volunteers to form a Thread Family that represents a diverse cross section of Baltimore. Volunteers work with trained volunteer coaches on how to connect with their young people and fellow volunteers to set goals, identify and remove barriers, and achieve their goals.

Thread commits to enrolled young people for ten years and has achieved 100 percent student retention since its founding in 2004. 79 percent graduate within six years of starting high school and 62 percent complete a two- or four-year degree or certification.

Thread plans to annually enroll 7 percent of Baltimore's high school freshmen to seed a movement of more than twenty thousand Baltimoreans working together to build a city where everyone can thrive.

It Takes a Village

Will Jackson

How can we create classrooms that all learners, including Black learners, can relate to and thrive in—and transform the education system in the process? Will Jackson shares his insights about the lived experience of Black learners, the assets and aspirations of Black parents, and the power of connections and collaborations. A conversation about culture, why our ideas of expertise need updating—and how we can all win.

Will, why is it important to look at education as a system, instead of just monitoring the performance of individual students?

Because the system is what's causing harm. I use the metaphor of fish and water. Let's say you arrive at a lake and you see that not one but all the fish are sick or dead. You probably will want to examine the water quality, right? Same with race and education—the problem is not within Black children, it's within a system that's disproportionately suspending them, disproportionately not recommending them for gifted or advanced classes, disproportionately not looking out for them when it comes time to prepare for college. A child can't fix this, a child can't say "put me in an AP course." The teachers, assistant principals, counselors are making those decisions. And they're often deciding, even if unconsciously, based on the kid's skin color. Some learners end up surviving anyway, but it almost always comes at some cost to their racial or cultural identity. The question is, is that even success?

You're working to create ideal learning environments for all learners, including Black learners. Why is culture your starting point?

Well, let's look at what learning is. It's the act of connecting prior knowledge to new information. And where does prior knowledge come from? It comes from your home, it comes from the people who raised you, it comes from the people who know you. That's culture. Prior knowledge is important for identity—but also for cognition. Now, close to 40 percent of K–12 students are Black and Brown kids—about 20 percent are Black kids. But 80 percent of the teachers in this country are white. That means it is very likely that the cultural knowledge a teacher relies on in the classroom does not match the prior knowledge Black children have. For example, teachers may use analogies or historical references that students miss completely. Not because they aren't smart or they don't care, but because it's outside the child's cultural experience. But instead, the narrative is "these kids come to school knowing nothing" or "their parents aren't invested in ensuring their children are school ready."

Can you give an example?

I remember going into a math class right after starting Village of Wisdom and seeing a wall of portraits of white guys who were being celebrated as the people who advanced math across the centuries. What this signaled to me— and I assume to Black students in general—was that people who look like us have nothing to contribute here. They give all the old white guys the credit. That approach is in stark contrast to how my mom, who was a teacher, brainwashed me into believing that all scientists were Black! Every time we talked about science at home, we talked about people like George Washington Carver, Benjamin Banneker, Dr. Mae Jemison, Dr. Charles Drew. So that was my prior knowledge about the history of science.

How does the atmosphere of school come across to a Black child who enters the classroom?

Black children have varied experiences, right? Some are going to all-Black schools, and they've got a lot of Black teachers, and maybe that's a positive experience. Some are going to more mixed schools where they might find a reasonably culturally affirming environment, and they're feeling decent about their identity, and they're learning. I'm not going to paint all schools as bad. And I'm definitely not going to paint them all as good. But I think what ends up happening more often than not is that many Black children are going into classroom experiences every day where teachers are demonizing their hair, their clothing, the way they talk. This has the effect of invalidating their home culture. For Black and Brown kids especially, we need to do a better job of recognizing that culture is essential to a child's development, learning, and sense of safety and belonging at school.

How can we change this? One resource you're tapping into is Black parents, right?

Correct. You know, I remember sitting in a classroom in grad school and a professor of mine telling me, "It won't be until Black parents decide that they've had enough that this country's schools will actually improve for Black children." Although I don't agree with putting so much onus on Black parents, her words stuck with me. Today, we have institutions trying to be more culturally responsive and affirming, but we can't build that kind of institution on the minds and ideas of people who are unfamiliar with the culture they are trying to support. We have to tap a different kind of expertise—an expertise more proximate to the culture of those we seek to benefit. For us at Village of Wisdom, that expertise comes from Black parents.

How do parents in your Village of Wisdom community engage with schools?

Initially we turned to research that says that Black parents are the ones most likely to buffer their kids from negative experiences at school. So we developed a framework, and this is still a central tool for us; it is called Black Genius framework. Our parents vow to protect and affirm the Black genius of their kids at home and at school. It's a strength-based, individualized tool that frames Black culture in positive ways. Any parent can go to our site right now and set up a profile for their child. You start with the Black Genius brainstorm that's a series of questions you can ask your child. How does he think about his Blackness? What are some of the cultural environments she moves across? What types of injustice is she most moved by? Who does he trust? Older students can do this on their own, of course. So this is a tool for parents and students to use on their own, then take to schools and teachers.

And by observing parents use the Black Genius framework, we were again reminded that Black parents have wisdom to offer teachers and school communities, and the education system as a whole. As educators of all races, creeds, colors, and genders are thinking about how to be responsive to all learners, they need parents who will counsel and guide them, collaborate with them, validate their approaches as being culturally affirming or not. I mean, I have small kids, so I'm a relatively new parent, but I've been Black my whole life. I have a lot to share with somebody who has not spent any time being Black. So now we're asking: What would it look like to engage Black parents as reflective practice partners to educators—at a time when we're all trying to create a better education system for all learners?

What does that kind of partnership look like? Are teachers receptive?

I think the good ones are. For example, we needed a reflective practice partner in one of our partner schools here in Durham, North Carolina, where I live and where our team is based. One of our parents turned out to be a great fit. She had two kids in that school, and she also has some training in education. So we reintroduced our Black Genius framework to her and

"Let's listen to Black parents, their concerns and ideas, and invite them to help our educational institutions get better. That's how we can imagine change happening in all our schools."

"For Black and Brown kids, we need to do a better job of recognizing that culture is essential to a child's development, learning, and sense of safety and belonging at school."

Will Jackson

prepared her to help the teachers figure out how to integrate the framework into their instructional decisions. People often assume that such a process will be adversarial, that even the relationship between teachers and parents has to be adversarial, right? But that's not the case. This mom was really helping these teachers. She advised them how to integrate our framework into their instructional practice. She reduced some of the teachers' sense of isolation that often comes when teachers take a more antiracist approach to teaching in this country. In fact, she helped the teachers in this small cohort build community among themselves. And the teachers, well, they are seeing the Black learners in their class succeed. This success is due to this new kind of partnership with Black parents that allowed them time, and space, with a Black parent being compensated, to help them think through the sometimes uncomfortable feelings and awkward approaches that come along with race-based conversations. This is the change we're looking for, right? So, coming back to your question whether teachers are receptive: I'd say for the teacher who has never had any intention of creating a more culturally affirmative environment for Black children, no, they're not going to want this. But for those teachers who do have that intention and are receptive to feedback, absolutely they will welcome this resource.

In some ways, you're flipping or expanding what counts as expertise, who an expert is. Do you see the landscape changing?

I do. When I first started talking about Black parents, they weren't really on anyone's radar. And they certainly weren't being looked to as experts. Even the idea of proximate leaders didn't get traction until recently, right? Which, by the way, I give Bryan Stevenson a lot of credit for championing that. I mean, it's pretty wild that we just tended to assume we can impose solutions from the top. It is repugnant that philanthropy has designated whole funding initiatives and invested millions and millions of dollars without ever talking to the people who've actually experienced the problem, without asking for their input or ideas.

The thing that folks need to understand about proximity is it reveals a nuance that people at a distance just can't have. It's like having a microscope that allows you to see things up close. So, bringing it back to education, what I'm asking is, what if we can apply these institutional resources, such as funds earmarked for education fellowships and so on, and invest some of that in an existing but newly appreciated group of experts, Black parents and other parents of color? Let's give them decision-making power. Let's listen to their concerns and their ideas and invite them to help our educational institutions get better equipped to offer liberatory possibilities to all children. That's how we can imagine change happening in all our classrooms, all our schools.

Village of Wisdom runs "dream assessments" for teachers and parents. Why is this important?

We have set up our education system to meet kids' needs, not necessarily to ask: Who do these kids want to be, what are their dreams? One of the questions we ask teachers is, "What are your dreams for Black children?"

If you are going to be teaching my child, I want to know if you have a dream in mind for them, right? When you ask a Black parent that question, that parent will go immediately to, "I want my kid to be the best they can possibly be. I want them to realize all of their own dreams. I want them to be able to live up to their full potential." It's on the tip of their tongue. They don't even have to think about it. But sometimes with teachers, you get a pause, like, "Hmm. I never thought about that." When you think of it, that is a bit heartbreaking. And as a parent, I'm being asked to trust my child to somebody who's going to be taking care of them, and they haven't necessarily thought, "What's my dream for this child?"

What recommendations would you give about hiring new teachers?

Well, if a teacher is going to work at an all-Brown school, for example, let's ask that teacher, what is your cultural familiarity with this group? Have you spent any time with folks in this community? Have you lived with, loved, cared for Brown kids? Have you lived with, loved, cared for Black children? These questions will crystallize whether someone has shown an interest before coming to teach these kids. And it can uncover the savior complex that sometimes drives teachers. I'm thinking right now about that Lilla Watson quote, "If you have come here to help me you are wasting your time, but if you have come because your liberation is bound up with mine, then let us work together." We want teachers who are motivated by this kind of idea, not by the idea of saving anybody.

More and more, schools are setting up equity and diversity teams and goals. Is this a hopeful sign?

Yes, but how it's being done is key. We're seeing a few layers of challenge having to do with leadership and accountability, strategies, and resource allocation. The main question schools need to be asking is: How do we create culturally affirming instructional environments? When we point this out, people sometimes come back to us with, "Well, we already had a day for Latinx history, or an Indigenous day." Or whatever it is. But unless these kinds of activities are connected to a clear strategy for addressing inequity, they are not helpful. Look, you have these kids in the classroom, they learn by connecting prior knowledge to new information, and if you're not talking about changing the instructional patterns inside your classroom, you are wasting time. We need to embed equity deeply into the process of creating learning environments, or it won't work.

Coming back to the philanthropic landscape and proximate leadership. In the past, only 4 percent of funding went to Black institutions. Are you seeing a change here?

Ha, well, I'm still finding this all somewhat triggering. Some three, four years ago, I found myself talking to a lot of institutions that would tell me they liked our know-how and approach, but that they would not be able to support our work because we didn't have "the institutional capacity." By that, they meant we weren't big enough. That we didn't have enough funding, didn't have enough staff members.

And then we could see them turn around and give funding to people who had all kinds of institutional capacity but no cultural expertise. And now, four years later, I find myself in this situation where these foundations and institutional folks who got all the funding, who supposedly have all this institutional capacity, come to us wondering what Black parents think, wondering what Black parents are going to do to organize, wondering whether we can help them explain to the world why we need to teach race in the classroom and push back against this critical race theory witch hunt—because somehow, many of the organizations philanthropy has invested in ain't got the guts to do that. And that's assuming they have the knowledge and skill.

Despite the lack of investment, Black organizations like ours have gotten by on a bare minimum to push the movement and the culture forward, to change the country, to make it better for everyone. And now dominant institutions are asking us for expertise, for insights, but never gave us the funding or the money or the resources that we asked for in the first place.

My question to philanthropy, to school boards, is: What happens when you actually start to believe in us? What happens when you actually give Black people the resources that we deserve? What happens when you actually make a moral decision to say, we're going to invest back into the Black community that for so long has done so much with so little?

And you know what?

What?

White folks have lost in all this, too. Part of the deal of whiteness was to give up your culture to assimilate to the white power structure. So Irish, Germans, Jewish people all became white to access power, and parts of their culture and their ethnic contributions were lost for the benefit of white power. But what happens when you trade your culture and traditions for power? What happens when your identity becomes synonymous with power and power alone? In many ways this reflection on the cost of assimilating to whiteness harkens back to the beginning of this interview: If your achievement comes at the sacrifice of your identity, then is that really success? And: As people created whiteness to maintain power, there was a whole narrative that had to be created to exclude and diminish the experience and contributions of Black and Brown folks. And now, as the truth about the contributions of Black and Brown people becomes harder and harder to ignore and cover up, white folks whose sole identity is tied to power are becoming anxious and afraid because their sense of self is being threatened. This leads to a key question: Who creates knowledge versus who is credited with creating knowledge? Whose voices are and have been left out of the conversation? What ramifications does this have for young people and all people who want to intellectually contribute to a just and free society?

Will Jackson spoke with Konstanze Frischen and Amy Clark.

Will Jackson is the founder of Village of Wisdom. The organization is mobilizing a nationwide movement of families to celebrate and protect their children's Black genius. Based in Durham, North Carolina, Village of Wisdom supports family organizing and advocacy entities with tools and resources that help parents, teachers, and students create affirming learning environments for Black and Brown learners, and protect the intellectual curiosity and positive racial self-concept of Black children through the love and wisdom of their families and communities.

We Belong Here

Angelou Ezeilo

The environmental sector in the U.S. is predominantly white. When Angelou Ezeilo set out to change this, she focused on opening up new career pathways for young people of color. But she soon realized that it would take more than supporting Black and Brown people to diversify the environmental movement. A conversation about history, outdoor recreation, power, and the privilege of roaming around freely.

Angelou, the U.S. is rich in natural beauty, has a unique system of national parks...but when it comes to the question of who is enjoying these spaces, who recreates in the outdoors, the numbers skew very heavily white.

Yes, they do. And there's a growing awareness right now that this is not because people of color are not interested in the outdoors. That's a biased assumption that you sometimes hear. The reality is much more complex than that, and it is dawning on people, especially since George Floyd got killed and Christian Cooper harassed—you know whom I'm talking about, right?

Yes, the Black man who was bird-watching in Central Park when he was harassed by a white woman who called the police on him under false pretense, which could likely have threatened his life.

Right. So in the wake of that incident—which happened the day George Floyd was murdered—the environmental world has been starting to wake up: "Holy cow, this is us as well." Of course, Black environmentalists knew that already. But the majority in the environmental sector didn't realize it until Christian Cooper was compounded by George Floyd: that it wasn't even safe for a birder and Harvard graduate to watch birds in plain daylight in the middle of Manhattan.

Which sounds so unbelievable.

And yet it is true. It all boils down to safety. Black people often do not feel safe in the outdoors, and for good reasons. And now those reasons are the lenses that environmental organizations are starting to look through. The sector has been so homogeneous, so white and male for so long, that we haven't seen much change in decades. The fact that it's finally starting to happen—slowly, but happening regardless—is progress. Which is all to say: Despite the challenges, it is an exciting time right now to be in the environmental space. To reimagine public land, to reimagine the outdoors. To ask the question: Who gets to sit at the table and to make the decisions that shape our public spaces?

You launched this work in 2007, when you set up the Greening Youth Foundation. Precise diversity numbers in the environment are really hard to come by, but according to a study conducted in 2014 of nearly three hundred environmental groups, including government agencies and grant-making foundations, the number of people of color on staff did not exceed 16 percent despite accounting for almost 40 percent of the population, and they were concentrated in the lower ranks—a vast underrepresentation, compounded by hierarchy. What tipped you off to start the journey to correct this?

As a kid, I spent my summers in upstate New Jersey, where my parents owned fifty-four acres of forested land, with a small farmhouse on it. And I loved it. But because of my skin color, my parents were not necessarily supportive of me pursuing a career in the environment. Nor were there any images of people in the field who looked like them or me. After a career in law, it did seem like a logical step to me, though, to switch sides and help a new generation embrace environmental stewardship. But you know what?

What?

For most years, at Greening Youth Foundation, we focused heavily on the supply side—Black and Brown kids. And we still do that. Starting with kindergarten age, we want to make sure that these kids from underrepresented, disenfranchised communities can experience open spaces, this magic of being out among trees and grass. It's so important that children can have this opportunity early on, to stimulate the desire in them to be out in nature. And then with older age groups, we give them the opportunity to embark on robust, supported career pathways in conservation. We invest in them, prepare them—teach them biology, forestry, trail restoration, teach them the language they'll need to know, the scientific concepts...everything so they can go on and successfully pursue internships with federal land management agencies like the National Park Service and secure a job in the conservation movement.

But then over the last five years, within our leadership team, we realized something was off. We had this epiphany, this moment of "Wait a minute! We are putting all this emphasis into changing the face of the environmental movement by preparing people of color and investing in them. But aren't we forgetting something?" Because it is not just these young people that we need to be working on. It's the organizations and entities that these young people are going to work with that need to shift, too! That's the other side of the coin.

Because unless you change the modus operandi of these institutions, people of color won't feel welcome there—won't feel safe even?

Exactly. Both sides need education. It's not just focusing on the fish, it's focusing on the water, too. It seems so obvious now, but it was really an "aha" moment. We were so brainwashed that we didn't really see it earlier.

And what made you see the situation differently?

Quite a number of the young people we were training had been met with such vitriol during their internships that it was causing them to go running, and telling people in their community and their churches and their schools, "Nah, that was not a good experience for me." And when we realized the extent of that...and when we started fielding more calls from parents who were concerned about their children...Oh my! It felt like years of our work went completely down the drain. That's when we shifted gears. We started calling our federal partners and environmental NGO partners and networks and said, "We need to have a conversation." And mostly, people there were not aware. There's so much unconscious bias. People are not aware how they are viewing other people who do not look like them. It's just now, after the Black Lives Matter movement, that this is becoming more obvious to more people, and it's easier to talk about it.

Let's stay there. Because this is going right to the heart of the issue: This is not just about any individual's behavior or bias; it's systemic, it's ingrained in culture. As you say, it's the water, not the fish. And that goes back a long time.

Yes. Who has the right to be and feel safe in what spaces. It goes back to Native Americans and how they were killed and driven off their land, and moves on to slavery, when Black people were kidnapped from one place and traded, and their movement, alongside their liberties, got cut down to the bare minimum, just so they would still be productive.

Recently, my children wanted to learn more about Harriet Tubman. So we went to the Harriet Tubman Underground Railroad Visitor Center on the Eastern Shore in Maryland, the region where she was born and to which she returned many times to guide more enslaved people to freedom. The museum is built right next to a national wildlife refuge and is surrounded by creeks and marshes. And this unbelievable discrepancy stood out: Here's this woman who's what we'd call an environmentalist and outdoor expert today. She has this deep knowledge of the region's flora and wildlife, she can navigate the waterways in harsh winters and hot summers, she navigates by the stars...and yet she isn't free to be in the spaces where she wants to be.

Exactly! I love it that you mention Harriet Tubman. We celebrate her as a Black environmentalist. And yes, totally, when she escaped, and on the Underground Railroad, she would have been captured and killed if she had not had knowledge of nature and how to navigate within it. This was of course true for enslaved people in general.

And this segregation in space, this redlining of nature, that would allow whites to be where they'd want to be but keep Blacks confined and fearing for their lives?

Absolutely! We all know about segregated buses and schools, but the segregation of the outdoors, the segregation of space, happened alongside that. I'm not sure many people have heard of the Green Book. It's a Black travel guide published during Jim Crow, for Black travelers, to inform which gas stations were friendly to Blacks, which hotels, which restaurants would serve them on road trips. Then of course there were sundown towns, where Blacks couldn't go. You get it again and again: a deeply ingrained cultural notion that people of color need to be confined and shouldn't be recreating or just even enjoying the outdoors the way the majority does.

Once you start seeing it, it's hard to unsee.

That segregation of the outdoors, or rather the linking of outdoors and white majority, was also baked into the New Deal, when Roosevelt created the Civilian Conservation Corps, which was meant to give millions of men employment in the conservation field during the Great Depression—they planted billions of trees and constructed trails and infrastructure in hundreds of parks across the U.S.

The intention was great. But then, in parts of the country—take Georgia, for instance—Black men were explicitly denied entry to the program. In counties with a majority of African Americans, 60 percent, this major segment of the population was excluded. And then despite an amendment outlawing racial discrimination, Black folks across the nation who wanted to do this work—building infrastructure, working on national parks, all these wonderful, important things—they had to live and work in separate camps, in segregated environments, which is absolutely ridiculous. And similarly, there was a separate CCC section for Native Americans. So in fact, Black people were excluded from the CCC, Native Americans were excluded, women were completely excluded. Institutional and cultural segregation were firmly planted, and the seeds of that we're still dealing with to this day.

So it is this history of confining the freedom of people of color, of confining their right to be where they want to be, that takes us right back to the settlers, to slavery, to Jim Crow, to sundown towns and the Green Book, to the CCC, and to Christian Cooper bird-watching in Central Park.

Yes. But the promising thing, which is what I always love coming around to, is that young people are the hope of tomorrow, in every sense of the word. Younger, diverse voices are moving in, and they are questioning the status quo. "Why is this the first time in fifty years that we have a woman that's being considered for that position?" "Why is there no single person of color in the leadership of this organization?" "Why is there less than 1 percent people of color on staff?" Across the board, folks are starting to notice that this is not normal.

This underrepresentation of people of color in the environmental field is especially striking because they have been disproportionately affected by climate change and environmental pollution.

Think of Hurricane Katrina and New Orleans, the water crisis in Flint...But now young people from these communities are raising their voices and starting to get engaged. I'm happy to say Greening Youth Foundation has been a big part of creating these young advocates and raising the level of environmental awareness. More and more, young people know: If there's a problem or an issue that is affecting their community, their environment, they can step up. They can join or lead a group, organize, campaign, help the effort to change the paradigm, change the narrative. And as part of our advocacy work, what we're saying is: You have to stay close to the people who are disenfranchised, marginalized. Because they are likely to be the most impacted. If you lose sight of that, what's affecting them the most, then you got to go back to the drawing board.

When white people are marching for social justice and expressing their angst about climate change, can that sometimes be perceived as overshadowing the fact that communities of color have been much harder hit by environmental pollution?

Well, as usual in conversations about diversity, equity, and inclusion, this can get really sticky. The baseline is: If we're talking about progressing as a human society, then any issue that is impacting one group should be impacting everybody—in terms of everybody feeling that this is not right. In other words, we all need to be allies. However, when any allied group turns it on themselves and makes themselves the focus, their angst, and how they're feeling as a result, then that's when it becomes a bit tricky. So that's why we advise young people to not lose sight of the ones impacted most. The ones with the lived experience must be able to speak. It's a little uncomfortable, but all of this stuff is uncomfortable. It's 2021, and we're still talking about race relations and why there aren't people of color in the environmental sector. That should be uncomfortable for everybody.

What's the role of empathy in these conversations?

That's the major factor. People being open. Try to learn about groups you don't know much about. Talk to them. Expand your social circle. Be friendly and open, research what their issues are, learn what they are fighting for in the legislature. Ideally, you can understand these issues from a personal perspective through somebody who has a lived experience. That will make all the difference in the world. That will help you understand why mothers of

Black boys have so much angst when they leave the house.

That's personal for you.

Yes, it is...I'm the mother of two Black boys—men really; they are men now.
Over six foot two. And here in the U.S., I feel like they are walking around
with targets on their back. Every single time, when they are home, when they
take our car, before they drive off and shout, "Oh, we'll be back in an hour,"
my husband and I, we feel something inside contracting, and we're often not
even aware of it. We talked about it the other day, he and I, how until we see
them pulling down the driveway, we don't feel relaxed. There's angst and
there is fear—because of wondering whether they're safe or not. This feeling
has definitely aided my desire to get them to another country. They are both
abroad now, at college, working. And this is really a sad commentary about
where we still are as a country. That's why our work is so complicated.

As you said earlier: It all boils down to safety.

It does. That's why some young people went running from their internships.
And why parents are still worried. They understand the career opportunity for their child. But they wonder whether it is safe for their daughter to
go to the Grand Tetons and spend the summer there if there's no one else
around that looks like her. So we have to mentor them and coach them—not
just the young people, but also the parents. That's why we still need a lot
of hand-holding on the way. Of course, the more young people of color go
there, the safer it becomes.

How are institutions changing?

Well, let's face it, there are still many people, older folks often in particular,
who do not want a whole lot of change. They say they do, but they don't,
because they feel threatened. I often come in personally—I feel like I'm a
bridge. I'm so connected to these young people, through Greening Youth,
my skin color, my lived experience. But I'm also of an older generation now, I
have to admit it. And I can see older folks wanting to know and feel that they
are still relevant. At this very micro level, we need to understand how we can
better work together. And mentorship can play an important role here—not

just the older person mentoring the younger one, but also the other way around.

It should be in their own self-interest, right?

Absolutely. Ultimately, at a higher level, organizations will need to change if they want to stay strategic. With the shifting demographics in the U.S., unless they diversify the makeup of their staff, they will become less relevant and less legit.

But let me tell you: I'm often asked whether I know a quick remedy. Yet for this cultural change to happen, to recruit and retain more people of color, everyone will need to play their part. I can support—I can provide reading material and learning opportunities and all that, so white folks can be self-reflective. But I cannot provide the quick remedy. This must come from their end as well.

Angelou Ezeilo spoke with Konstanze Frischen.

Angelou Ezeilo is the founder of the Greening Youth Foundation. The Greening Youth Foundation (GYF) is cultivating a generation of youth of color to be stewards of land and natural resources, ultimately aiming to shift the demographics of the environment conservation movement.

GYF provides environmental education for underserved K–12 students, college internships in natural resource fields, and hard and soft skills training for green jobs. These opportunities increase student knowledge of the environmental field, expose them to role models already working in the sector, and provide job training, work experience, and career entry points into the conservation field.

From its home base in Atlanta, Georgia, GYF provides programming to over five thousand children, youth, and young adults annually. In 2019–2020 GYF managed over four hundred interns and service crew members in thirty-one states, Washington, D.C., Guam, Puerto Rico, and the Virgin Islands, as well as Ghana, Lesotho, Liberia, and Nigeria. Founded in 2007 as an all-volunteer organization active in elementary schools in Gwinnett County, Georgia, Greening Youth has grown to a staff of eighteen full-time employees. In addition to its Atlanta office, GYF currently maintains a country office in Lagos, Nigeria.

Building Community Wealth

Tim Lampkin

How can we close the racial wealth gap? Start by making it easier for Black Americans to access capital and build assets, says Tim Lampkin. A conversation about expanding Black business ownership across the Mississippi Delta, reimagining collateral, and why poverty is not an outcome of individual choices, but a function of a biased system.

Tim, you live in an iconic place, the Mississippi Delta. Can you tell us a bit about it?

I'd love to. I'm proud to have been raised here in the Delta—these eighteen counties in the northwest part of the state. It's primarily flat lands with fertile soil, and agriculture is one of the main industries. Many musicians, artists, and creatives live here, some of them known all over the world. And it's also home to great Americans who moved the country forward, like Fannie Lou Hamer, Aaron E. Henry, Vera Mae Pigee, Reubin Smith, Unita Blackwell, Isaiah T. Montgomery.

And yet, when we hear about Mississippi in the news, the story is often less positive. Why is that?

Everyone leads with the negative aspects, right? They talk about racism. They talk about the schools. They talk about poverty. And then, now and then, they sprinkle in, "But oh, that's the birthplace of the blues, and I love blues music, and I love the food there." I don't overlook the negative things that happened here and still happen here—I mean, there are people in my family who remember picking cotton for thirty cents a day, big bags of cotton, and they're out there for hours in the heat. So that's part of our history. But what's also part of our history is the civil rights movement, and all the progress we've made.

Here's an example. Maybe you followed the debate about our Mississippi state flag, the old one with the Confederate battle sign on it? The media covered it for years, a decade. Well, we finally have a new flag—but now that it's good news, a sign of progress, no one's paying attention. I'm not saying that reckoning shouldn't happen, because it should, but I hope we'll also learn to celebrate wins and lift them up as part of our story going forward. If we're going to talk about Mississippi, or any other place, let's talk about it completely: what's broken and what solutions are actually working.

And in your case, you are working to correct wealth inequalities stemming from systemic racism and underinvestment in Black communities. What do people misunderstand about the racial wealth gap?

The main misunderstanding is around why it exists. The reality is that Black families in America, and particularly those in many parts of the South, have been excluded for generations from opportunities to build wealth—to access education, buy homes, start businesses. And before that, we were enslaved people. So, it can get tiring to hear things like, "Well, why can't people just pull themselves up by their bootstraps?" Too many people still think that Black poverty is a personal choice. When I'm asked about this, I ask back: "Do you think people who are poor want to be poor? Do you think a single mom wants to be working three jobs and not spending time with her family?" We need equal opportunities for all people and reparations for Black Americans.

How has this understanding of the origins of the wealth gap influenced your work?

Black residents are almost 40 percent of the population of Mississippi. And yes, there is work to be done to close the racial wealth gap here. So, in 2016, we started our organization, Higher Purpose Co., to try to get things moving in a new direction. Now we work with two hundred Black entrepreneurs, farmers, and artists in our business membership. Most of our members identify as Black women, many of them single mothers starting businesses to increase their monthly income—and equal pay for women is still a major issue here. Our farmers are typically mature in age and experience, less often young people, due to the stigma of working on land associated with the cotton industry and slavery. Artists in our membership include photographers, painters, and musicians. Now, five years in, we're seeing our business members exchanging expertise, mentoring each other, doing business together.

How does Higher Purpose Co. help its members build wealth?

We lower barriers to creating viable businesses, so our members can build up their assets over time. Now, most of our members do not have family wealth to draw on. Most are first-time entrepreneurs seeking at least $10,000 to support their business. We offer a continuum of capital to get businesses the funding they need to move forward. We do this by leveraging business growth grants, individual development accounts, equity investments, loan guarantees, zero-interest Kiva loans, and low-interest loans from community development financial institutions, plus traditional loans from larger banks.

We also leverage our loan guarantee pool to help if there is a shortage of collateral. And—and this is very important—we try to avoid asking for any personal collateral.

Why is this important?

Well, for centuries, the labor of Black people, our ancestors, created wealth for white people and institutions in Mississippi and across the country. So, when these institutions ask us to provide collateral to borrow money from the wealth Black people created, it is very extractive. So, we've been really challenging ourselves and our partners to reimagine collateral and put some parameters around it to protect our business owners. In most cases, we do our best to remove personal collateral like homes and cars from the conversation. We focus instead on other kinds of collateral like equipment and buildings that, if lost, would not impinge on someone living their life. We do not want somebody's home to be leveraged to start a business when the whole point is to build family and community wealth.

So, by working with these entrepreneurs, having a support system for them, and leveraging these different types of capital, we're able to reduce the financial risk for everybody involved, including traditional lenders. At the end of the day, we are advocates for our entrepreneurs. We get the financial institutions to do what they do best, then we come in and do what we do best, which is supporting the entrepreneurs along their journey.

Banks have been making big commitments this year to addressing the racial wealth gap. What are they getting right, and what do they have to learn?

We work with a lot of financial institutions, and many have great lending products. What's missing is the conversation with the potential borrower. Let's say you are a bank creating a new loan product because you want to support more Black-owned businesses. Have you talked to Black business owners? Have you asked them what they actually need to move their businesses forward? The other aspect we need to reimagine is true community engagement, because having a physical branch in an area doesn't mean you have a community connection. That's why we invite lenders to come to talk

"Have you talked to Black business owners? Have you asked them what they actually need to move their businesses forward?"

"Do you think people who are poor want to be poor? Do you think a single mom wants to be working three jobs and not spending time with her family?"

Tim Lampkin

to us and our members. We will help you develop products and plans that respond to what Black entrepreneurs need to succeed.

Earlier you mentioned community development financial institutions (CDFIs) that invest public funds alongside private capital to build stronger communities—are they allies?

Yes. CDFIs are mandated by the government to reach underserved communities, and we're encouraged to see new federal funds flowing to these lenders. With these new allocations, CDFIs are now more than ever obligated to get funds out the door fast. This can translate into funding large business deals that may absorb a lot of capital but may not address underlying inequities. There's actually no shortage of capital in Mississippi. The problem is access to capital—a key issue when it comes to addressing the racial wealth gap.

So, my question is about accountability and ensuring that the capital goes where it's needed most for change in the long run. For example, we still see white-owned businesses getting funded over Black-owned businesses simply because they can show assets to secure the loan—not because they are necessarily more creative or innovative. On top of that, the solutions we need here in Mississippi might be very different from those needed in, say, Arkansas or Louisiana, or other states in the Deep South. Take some of our rural communities in Mississippi, where most folks don't have many assets. If financial institutions, including CDFIs, are practicing the status quo, if they are using traditional loan products, they are missing the opportunity. They need to reassess and say, "Hey, how can we co-create a loan process and a product that can help us get this money out to people who really need it?"

On this point about adaptability, what did the pandemic reveal about financial institutions and their responsiveness to borrowers?

It caused financial institutions to adjust, and some of what shifted was very positive, worth keeping and building on. Like lower interest rates and closing costs for some groups. And deferred loan payments for three to six months. So, the conversation we're having with some of our partners is: Why did it take a global crisis to change things that weren't working anyway for our borrowers? What should we implement permanently? Looking ahead, there's also an opportunity to do things like streamline the loan application process, so that it's competitive but not duplicative. We've seen this process be very tiresome for a lot of our entrepreneurs.

You made recommendations for the Community Reinvestment Act (CRA), the federal act that requires financial institutions receiving federal funds to reinvest a portion of profits into community health and wealth—what did you propose?

We wanted to discuss payday lenders. Some states have completely abolished them, but many have not. Where I live, for example, you'll find more payday lenders on Main Street than banks. And these lenders are very predatory. They'll charge interest rates as high as 400 percent or more, and they use vicious intimidation tactics. If you don't pay on time, people call your workplace, repossess the collateral. On the flip side, though, they welcome everyone without bias. Some banks may greet a borrower with, "We'll be with you in a few minutes," and that few minutes may turn into a longer wait time if you're Black and seeking a business loan. Well, that same borrower can go right up a street to the payday lender and be welcomed with open arms. "You have bad credit? Great. We can still help you. Here's $5,000 today." There is something very flawed in a financial system that makes it expensive to be poor. So let me be clear: I'm speaking from my actual lived experience growing up in poverty, and this is why I don't think payday lenders should exist in our country. But if we can't get rid of them, let's hold them accountable and require them with policy to invest back into the community, like other CRA-mandated financial institutions are required to do.

The racial wealth gap has hardly budged in decades. How optimistic are you about the opportunity right now?

I think the next five years will be critical if we're to take advantage of the energy and momentum that's happening right now. I'm not talking about politics or who's in office. I'm talking about everyday people who've had an awakening over the last eighteen months and now they're wrestling with what they can do. They are asking themselves, "How can I show up differently in my community, my company, my neighborhood, my church, my kid's school?" Some of these conversations have happened before, of course, but not at this scale. We'll also need to see systems-level disruption across many systems—housing, education, health. Otherwise, we'll find ourselves celebrating progress in one area, then the same day, a crazy housing bill or voting rights bill comes out that's a huge setback. Now is the time to overly fund Black-led organizations working to close the racial wealth gap, in addition to addressing other social and economic justice issues.

What challenges to progress do you anticipate?

We'll need to stay focused on the long view and be able to recognize when distractions are moving us away from systemic change. For example, I'm seeing some of the reactions to Juneteenth becoming a national holiday, and my fear is that this might become another way to commercialize yet another Black experience. Will we see big corporations coming out with Juneteenth sales, just like we have Labor Day and Fourth of July sales? Will Black Americans go spend our money with these larger companies due to how things are marketed to us as a demographic? A demographic with a lot of purchasing power, by the way. On the other hand, it does remind us of the power of policy. Two years ago, Juneteenth becoming a national holiday wasn't on many people's radar, except those who were active advocates. Now we have a federal holiday. So, it reminds us that in some ways, democracy works. Does it work for everyone? That's the question. Meanwhile, there are several policies that people have fought for, even died for, this last year, that didn't make it to see the light of day. Voting rights is a big one, and in many southern states, we're backtracking.

What about the promise for democracy on a local scale?

This is where I see a lot of opportunity. The questions I'm drawn to right now are: What can be sustained locally when it comes to addressing the racial wealth gap? When the administration in the White House changes, how can we ensure that what's created locally continues to grow? How can we take responsibility in the roles that we play, whatever sector we're in, to create new norms and policies that make resources equally available to everyone? Focusing on your local community, finding ways to highlight its uniqueness— this can grow into a broader strategy. We are seeing this across the country. Here in our community, for example, Higher Purpose Co. is creating a regional community wealth hub that will help us generate new energy and reframe how people think about Mississippi—and in particular how people think about Black people in the Mississippi Delta.

And what do you hope will have changed in, say, ten years?

I hope that affordable capital will be available for everybody, that the conversation around collateral will be completely different, that many more businesses here in the Delta will be run by Black people. I hope that disparities around the racial wealth gap will have shifted and that we will see an uptick in Black wealth, with many more people and families able to buy land, buy homes, invest in their children's education, and reinvest back into the community.

Tim, circling back to your point about the momentum for change right now, and the roles people can play, do you have any advice for people trying to navigate conversations across divides, conversations with people who don't see the world as they do?

Civil discourse can be very helpful. What I try to do is that I don't jump in explaining myself first. I try to start from a place of listening, of curiosity about why people believe the things they do, what has shaped their viewpoint. I ask—and I'm sincere, too—"Oh, you feel that way? Tell me more about that." I listen, then I try to help by adding new information, a new angle. And for me, it's a worthwhile conversation even when someone says, "I may not agree with you, but I understand where you are coming from and why you are doing this work."

Tim Lampkin spoke with Michael Zakaras and Amy Clark.

Tim Lampkin is the founder of Higher Purpose Co., an economic justice nonprofit started in 2016 and based in Clarksdale, Mississippi. The organization's mission is to build community wealth for Black residents in Mississippi, supporting the ownership of financial, cultural, and political power. Higher Purpose Co.'s theory of change is anchored by business ownership, narrative change, and advocacy. Higher Purpose Co. seeks to unapologetically tackle generational poverty, structural inequality, and institutional racism by utilizing solutions-based organizing. It works to support Black-owned businesses in ways that counter extractive capitalism, promoting regenerative business development instead. Higher Purpose Co. is the only Black-led statewide membership-based organization in Mississippi, providing over two hundred Black entrepreneurs, farmers, and artists with business education, funding, and advising.

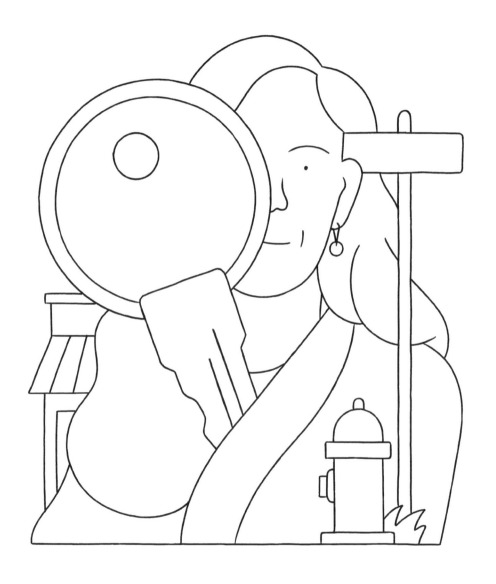

Toward an Ownership Economy

Alison Lingane

There is a near universal concern about the growth of wealth inequality in the U.S. So what are doable, practical pathways for creating better jobs, sharing profits, and keeping small businesses alive and jobs local? Let's focus on ownership, not just wages, says Alison Lingane. A conversation about solutions with political appeal for all sides, and the opportunity to build a more equitable economy.

Alison, there's a demographic shift happening in America that you think could have implications for the future of our economy and in particular our growing wealth gap.

Yes. Baby boomers are reaching retirement age in huge numbers—people refer to it as the "silver tsunami." They are an entrepreneurial generation. And nearly 2.5 million of them who still own the businesses they started decades ago are retiring now or will retire over the next ten to fifteen years.

That is huge—and not something we hear much about.

Exactly. This group of business owners owns one in two local businesses with employees in America. Not the multinational chain stores, but locally owned businesses that create jobs, from consumer-facing stores and restaurants to plumbers and electricians, local manufacturers or warehouse and shipping companies.

And the central question is: What will happen to these businesses? Succession planning is perpetually on tomorrow's to-do list for most business owners, but even those who are thinking about it only consider the options of finding a big buyer (which is hard to do), passing to your children (most kids don't take over their parents' businesses these days), or quietly closing down. We're coming to them with another option: sell to your employees.

What do you say to business owners?

We start by asking them: What's the legacy you want to leave, and what is the best way to achieve it? We share that employee ownership transitions allow you to stay in the driver's seat in terms of the timeline, process, how the transition goes—far more so than when you sell to a buyer you don't know. We share that with tax breaks, you can end up with more money in your pocket than from a traditional sale. Many business owners we partner with ultimately say: "Many of my employees have been here for ten or twenty years. They know the ins and outs. They understand the value. I would rather have this process play out so that they can carry on into the next generation."

And that decision gives employees a real stake in these companies going forward.

Yes. Employee ownership is an opportunity for people who work for businesses to be able to become owners of those businesses. That means reaping the financial benefits and the other benefits of having more voice and agency as an owner in that workplace. It means across our economy an opportunity to replace crappy jobs with good jobs.

What do you mean exactly when you say "crappy jobs"?

I mean jobs where someone is working full-time and can't make ends meet. Unfortunately, a growing number of jobs in this country would fall into that category. Today, 53 million working Americans (44 percent of all workers) qualify as "low-wage." People are working but have little opportunity to work their way up. Instead they fall further and further behind. There was a study done several years back that found that every new tech worker in the Bay Area creates five low-wage service jobs—someone to clean their house, take care of their kids, cook food in restaurants, drive them around.

You know, during the pandemic we heard a lot about "essential workers"— but are we paying them appropriately? We say we love them, but they are living on the edge with few pathways for advancement.

In fact, the pandemic has highlighted just how broken our economy is at a fundamental level. Income inequality is shocking. 40 percent of U.S. families are poor or low-income. About ninety million people had difficulty covering basic expenses in December of 2020.

But wealth inequality is even more shocking, and this is the gap that really holds people back, that is so hard to overcome in a low-wage job, and that with just a little bit of improvement, can make such a tremendous difference. The bottom 50 percent owns 2 percent of all wealth, while the top 5 percent owns a staggering 67 percent of all wealth. So we've got high-wage earners who are not only much higher in wages, but also much higher in wealth. And then we've got everybody else. That's our economy right now. Looking at these stats by race and ethnicity: according to inequality.org, the median wealth of Black families is just over $3,500, which is just 2 percent of the median wealth of white families (whose median wealth is nearly $147,000). Latino families aren't much better off, with median wealth of just over $6,500, which is 4 percent of the median wealth of white families.

Meanwhile, privately owned local businesses that have historically been an incredibly important part of our economy and communities are disappearing. On the consumer side: cafés replaced by Starbucks, independent food stores and barbershops replaced by chains. On the business-to-business side, private equity and publicly traded companies have been buying up whole sectors. So, this middle part of the economy where opportunity has historically been available is disappearing.

Why is employee ownership an antidote to these trends?

Well, it's better for both workers and businesses! Study after study demonstrates the benefits to workers and the success of employee-owned businesses—including a study conducted during the pandemic that showed the resiliency of such businesses compared with peers in their industry. Employee-owned enterprises were less likely to lay off employees and quicker to hire them back. They were more creative and agile in adapting to the sudden changes the pandemic required.

Can you give us an example?

Yes, there's a company in Northern California called California Solar Electric Company, one of our clients, that does solar design and installation. It's a company of about forty people. Right at the start of the pandemic they put all their workers on furlough to enable them to tap unemployment. Now, in a normal company, people on furlough are just on furlough, right? But Cal Solar employee-owners saw furlough as an opportunity to figure out what the heck to do with their business and get them out of furlough as quickly as possible. They came together and within months had figured out a whole new line of business, which was to become battery resellers—a growing market in California because of wildfires and power outages. And as battery resellers, they not only made up all of their lost revenue but actually grew their team and increased their wages by over 20 percent since becoming employee-owned.

So as you say, this was good for the business and for its workers.

The benefits of employee ownership for workers are many: A study by the National Center for Employee Ownership showed that wages on average are a third higher and assets as measured by household net worth are nearly twice as high as compared with workers within the same industry but not in employee-owned companies. Job stability is about 50 percent higher.

So, through employee ownership, people are staying in their jobs longer, they are earning more, they are building nest eggs and starting to chip away at intergenerational poverty. And ultimately, they are reviving what is left of the American Dream, especially for those at the bottom of the pay scale.

Imagine a low-wage worker having $100,000 or $200,000 of retirement assets. It's transformational. Especially when you think about the huge proportion of the workforce that has little to no savings—and about 40 percent of Americans can't afford a $400 unexpected car or medical bill.

What about the racial wealth gap in America?

That's a central reason for our existence—our organization's name is Project Equity. If you look at the demographics of our low-wage workforce, it is dominated by workers of color. And for many reasons, including structural racism that goes back to our country's founding, most business owners are white. The opportunity to transition ownership and build wealth is enormous from the standpoint of combatting the racial wealth gap—which, by the way, is just as big today as it was in 1968. The effects of closing that gap would ripple across generations in a completely game-changing way.

We have seen firsthand how shared business ownership translates to real money for low-wage workers and workers of color in the companies that we have helped. Profit-sharing that equates to a 30 percent increase over a $15 minimum wage for bakery workers. Half a million earned over two years by thirty pizzeria workers. In companies that are 100% employee-owned. These small businesses have transferred ownership and become wealth-generating engines for low-wage workers.

Do the benefits of an ownership economy extend into other areas—even civic participation and democracy?

There was a study from a few years back that correlated employee ownership with higher rates of voting. And that makes logical sense, right? People who are asked to bring their voices and be fully engaged in the workplace are more engaged in their communities, too. They have more agency in all aspects of their lives. More of a sense of self-determination. Imagine being invited to the board of directors of the company you work for. Suddenly you are given the right to show up in a position of authority, a position of power. And that can have a ripple effect outside the workplace.

I want to share a quick story. We were speaking with a company not long ago where the staff was bilingual. Many were native Spanish speakers. One gentleman who was a native Spanish speaker raised his hand and asked: "What about for somebody like me, who has an eighth-grade education? What does employee ownership mean for people like me, and how do you expect us to do this?" And it was a poignant moment because the answer is: That's the whole point of employee ownership. It can be for everyone. This gentleman might have an eighth-grade education, but he is smart and motivated and knows this company better than most people. The whole point is to build workplaces that meet people where they are and that prevent them from feeling like they don't belong, like they are on the outside looking in.

That's very powerful. And it begs the question: Given all these benefits, why isn't employee ownership the norm?

That is the central question. Jared Bernstein, who is a member of Biden's economic advisory team, had that same question and did a research study to try and answer it. And his grand conclusion, which we absolutely agree with in our work at Project Equity, is that it's lack of awareness . Employee ownership is unfamiliar to most. How many people do you know who work in employee-owned companies? So you get this phenomenon of "Well, since I haven't heard of it, it must not be any good." But that's starting to change. Congress passed the Main Street Employee Ownership Act in 2018 under a Republican-controlled House and Senate, to educate about succession planning and incorporate employee-ownership supports into the Small Business

Administration's programs, but there's a lot more to do to realize its potential. State and local governments have a big stake in this because they want to preserve jobs locally and keep their economy vibrant and unique and not just full of national chain stores. We know that employee-owned companies reinvest three times the number of dollars into the local economy as other businesses. So for states and cities, their own tax revenues are at stake. It's the difference between thousands of their businesses shutting down and relocating, or staying local for the next generation. We show them the data and watch them have the big "aha" moments. That is helping them to approach things with a certain urgency and recognize the opportunity window we have here.

How many employee-owned companies exist in the United States?

Only about seven thousand. It's a drop in the bucket, a rounding error. In other parts of the world it is much more common.

Is this because it gets labeled as being "socialist" here?

I think that does play a role. But we also have a lot of hero worship here in the U.S. around the sole entrepreneur. Look at how much media coverage there is of "self-made" billionaires here: "Look at what Elon Musk is up to now!" So there is a cultural element that has hampered the interest in and growth of this model.

And there is a lot of misunderstanding of employee ownership, too, right? What are some of the most common?

Yes. We talk a lot about the myths of employee ownership, and in addition to raising awareness we spend a lot of time doing myth busting. One of the most common myths is that employee-owned means that all employees have equal decision-making rights—in other words, every decision including what toilet paper to stock would require a vote. That's not true. Employee-owned companies also have management teams and CEOs or general managers, and while they are more informed by participatory management practices, they aren't going to employees for every decision. Another misconception is where the money comes from. In truth, employees do not need to finance the purchase of the business themselves.

Let's say I am a seventy-year-old business owner, and maybe this is my family's business, I'm second or third generation, and I'm looking to sell my company and retire. I might think: "Well, my employees could never buy my business from me; they don't have the money." But it's not financed by employee savings or their rich uncles, but rather by the future profits of the business itself.

How does that work exactly?

Let's say a business is worth $1 million (though it could just as easily be $10 million, or $100 million). For the sale, the business itself—not the employees—would take out a loan for say $700,000 from a bank that they pay to the seller. Meanwhile the seller grants a loan to the business for the remaining $300,000, which will paid back over five years via company profits. On the day of the sale, the seller will walk away with $700,000, and over the course of five years they would get the remainder with interest.

And then starting in year six, that profit that had been going to pay back the loan, that profit is now available to help the business to have additional money to invest to help it grow and be successful. And of course to share profits with the employee-owners.

How do you appeal to traditional economists and to conservatives? To those who might associate employee ownership with the hippie organic food store at the edge of town?

We lead with the preservation of our small business economy in the United States. Everyone cares about that—even more so after the pandemic and increased concerns about the vulnerability of our manufacturing supply chain or the ability to ramp up food production or PPE production on a regional level.

Hyper consolidation in our economy is actually a vulnerability. So it matters from a national security perspective. Losing local ownership—or for that matter, U.S. ownership—is a problem we can rally people around.

I want to add that one of the beautiful things about employee ownership is that it does cross the aisle. It makes sense, it's logical, it's not politically driven. Republicans love it. Democrats love it, perhaps for slightly different reasons. But it allows us to build from our commonality—from our shared aspirations of wanting to be able to make ends meet after working an honest day's work, to have some savings and financial cushion, to do better than our parents, to be able to send our kids to college, to retire with some stability.

What's most energizing to you these days?

Talking with business owners. Hearing their incredible life stories about their thirty- or forty-year-old endeavors, what it means to them personally, what they have learned and overcome in those decades. You can really sense the legacy that the baby boomers—this highly entrepreneurial generation—has in the business community and our local economies. You can sense the desire to hold on to that legacy and turn it into something that can continue to be of benefit to their local communities and to millions of employees moving forward into the next generation.

Alison Lingane spoke with Michael Zakaras and Amy Clark.

Alison Lingane is the co-founder of Project Equity. The organization is a national leader in the movement to harness employee ownership to maintain thriving local business communities, honor selling owners' legacies, and address income and wealth inequality.

With an explicit focus on low-wage workers and workers of color, Project Equity's vision is to shift employee ownership from "best-kept secret" to the mainstream. By tapping the "silver tsunami" of retiring business owners—a demographic shift that represents the biggest wealth transfer in our nation's history—its strategy creates real, lasting change by shaping the market of business transitions and impacting the systems that support them.

Since 2014, Project Equity has worked with partners around the U.S. to develop regional and national ecosystems that raise awareness about employee ownership as a local business retention tool, an exit strategy for business owners, and an impactful approach for addressing the wealth gap in the U.S. Project Equity provides hands-on consulting and transaction financing to companies that want to transition to employee ownership, as well as to the new employee-owners to ensure that they, and their businesses, thrive after the transition.

Getting to Zero

Rosanne Haggerty

Fighting homelessness is expensive: Pre-pandemic, the U.S. was already spending $12 billion annually on emergency responses to homelessness—without much impact, or worse perhaps: without any expectation of impact. We can do so much better, says Rosanne Haggerty. A conversation about the relevance of real-time data, what we can learn from public health, and the importance of setting ideological battles aside in order to focus on the task at hand.

Rosanne, as we were preparing for our conversation, it struck us that the vernacular is "the homeless," as if we were talking about one homogenous group. Now, you use the phrase "people experiencing homelessness," which implies homelessness being both separate from the person and being a transient state. Why does that matter?

Well, one of the principal misconceptions and barriers to progress in my field is this habit of thinking of those experiencing homelessness as a homogenous group. Let's use the analogy of a health crisis. When someone is sick, we know that could mean any number of things, and we can't really determine what's going on without an individual diagnosis. And the same is true for a housing crisis. The fact that a whole group of individuals and families who find themselves in a housing crisis are assumed to be similar or to have experienced the same thing is wrong. It is even dangerously wrong. Because it conflates many different challenges into one identity, which makes it harder for communities to actually get traction on solving the problem.

A key piece of what you have learned over the years is that in order to successfully reduce homelessness, it is imperative for communities to know every person experiencing homelessness by name and to have real-time information on their whereabouts.

Yes, communities need to understand those experiencing homelessness in their individuality and the specific ways in which they're experiencing a housing crisis. But the real breakthrough in our work with communities has been to look at the individual person and to look at the overall population pattern. What are the trends? Is the community's response actually leading to reductions in homelessness? What strategic interventions work? How can the community organize its activities and resources in a rigorous, nimble way to make homelessness rare overall and brief when a housing crisis does occur?

Tell us!

Right. Well, it might be helpful to start with something that is in some ways very obvious but has been hard to get at. Which is: Homelessness is a dynamic problem. It's not a static problem. People transition in and out of it. But for years, the assumption has been different. In the United States, the accepted measure of the number of those experiencing homelessness has been a once-a-year, end-of-January, anonymized estimate, and then the data comes out about fourteen months later. It tells you for instance that 17 out of 10,000 people experienced homelessness in January 2019. In reality, numbers move and change in every community on a daily basis. A game-changing shift is to make homelessness in any community completely visible in close to real time. That enables those engaged in the issue in any community to see things in a new way, to see the patterns of inflow and outflow on at least a monthly basis.

Second, we learned that communities must break that data apart to see what is causing people to become homeless. Are they returning to homelessness after being assisted in the past, and did that housing solution fall apart? Have they come back onto the radar screen of that community's homelessness response system after having possibly attempted to resolve the problem themselves? Are they experiencing homelessness for the first time, and what was the triggering event? That data begins to reveal the multifaceted challenges, in every individual and household's life, and to show the underlying pattern of what's driving increases or decreases in homelessness across a community. Without that kind of dynamic data, any community can just be guessing at what's going on—unable to know which of their interventions works or where they should be focusing their efforts to have the greatest impact.

You have spoken about homelessness as a public health crisis—has the pandemic helped people better grasp that analogy?

Yes, I do think so. Worldwide, with COVID, we are seeing the importance of data to create a shared picture of a challenge, to understand where the greatest risks are, to guide behavior and types of responses, and to assess what's working to reduce overall risk. The same is true for homelessness. We need a similar mindset, data tools, and population-level focus.

But of course, as in health, we also need the individual diagnoses of the barrier to stable housing to respond effectively to each individual's situation. For instance, it can be misleading and not helpful for understanding the nature of any public health problem to think in terms of averages. We must focus on specifics. When averages come into play—as in how long on average is it taking us to get someone rehoused; can we do that within thirty days or four months?—we'll need to also ask: Are there some outliers? It is not acceptable to say, "Oh, our average length of homelessness in our community is four months." Well, that could mean every person of color is actually experiencing homelessness for eight months, and every white person is experiencing homelessness for a couple of days.

The specificity, and the ability to disaggregate data, is critical in order to take accountable action and find equitable solutions to any challenge. We see that over and over again: very robust, very specific, and real-time data is essential to resolving homelessness and any public health crisis.

What does the reader need to know about what causes an individual or a family to become homeless?

It is a variety of things, coupled with poverty and weak social networks. Transitions are very vulnerable times, especially coming from institutions such as foster care, the criminal justice system, a hospitalization. Certainly, there are high rates of behavioral health challenges especially among the chronically homeless, meaning that the individual has been homeless a year or more and has a disabling condition. There are obviously financial reasons that lead people to experience homelessness, and family violence is frequently a factor. But the important takeaway is that these crises—with known risks of homelessness—should not lead to homelessness. Homelessness exists in wealthy countries because we have not chosen to organize our safety net system to prevent and end it, despite enormous amounts of money being spent. Homelessness is the result of this broken system.

Where does this broken system manifest itself?

One of the things that should be emphasized is that across the United States—and this was pre-pandemic, so not including the significant emergency and stimulus funds that have come into play since—more than $12 billion was being spent annually on emergency responses to homelessness. In other words: It's not as though the country isn't spending resources—but it is spending resources almost without any expectation of ending homelessness. This is an industry ripe for disruption.

You are saying the fact that homelessness still exists to the extent it does has less to do with how much we spend, and more with how we spend it?

Correct. We must ask ourselves these questions: What if we're not dealing primarily with a money problem? What if—in many communities—we do not even have a housing supply problem?

Now—on the coasts and in very high-cost cities, homelessness is a problem that is meaningfully exacerbated by high housing costs. But that tends to blur the fact that in a very significant part of the country, it's not the lack of availability of housing. Instead, it may be lack of coordination. With better data, communities can surface better questions, for example: What part of homelessness in our community is actually about housing supply? What part of it is the really inefficient use of public resources—endless emergency responses as opposed to coordinating around how to prevent homelessness or get each person or family out of the hamster wheel of living in a prolonged state of housing crisis? Why is it that the only help available for a household in a housing crisis typically becomes available after they become homeless?

How does the conversation about homelessness fall along the political spectrum? As in, do people on the right tend to assume that people who are homeless have made bad choices, whereas progressives say it's the system?

Let me say this: It's very hard to find anyone who's advocating for doing nothing about homelessness. In our work, we have not met that person. What's missing is a sense of accountability for solving the problem—and a really deep understanding of what's going on. As we discussed earlier, there are many misconceptions to overcome. On the left, you'll frequently hear statements like—and I'm overdrawing this now, just to illustrate—"We need to spend more money on homelessness" or "It's all about more affordable housing: Let's pass another bond issue."

On the right, you do have some pushback around "housing first," a very critical principle which means housing assistance is not conditional on behavior. The well-documented truth is that no one is going to recover from a health or a mental health condition or from substance abuse if they remain homeless. Thus, there is the practice of providing housing as the first step in assisting someone experiencing homelessness in getting their life back on track. Once in stable housing, other supports—health, mental health, employment—are made available to help people get back into the flow of their lives in an environment of dignity and support. But as I said, there is a school of thought on the right which is very challenging of "housing first," seeing it as rewarding bad behavior and arguing for withholding housing assistance until addictions or mental health crises are resolved.

But what's interesting is that while opposition to "housing first" often comes from right-of-center faith-based groups, you also have groups on the left who don't think of themselves as being "anti–housing first," but who consistently make choices to exclude people from their services—people whom they see as difficult or not conforming with the design of their programs. The effect of these exclusionary practices on those experiencing homelessness is the same.

In other words: Things are more complex than they appear.

Yes. I'd say the most extreme and least helpful narrative—and one that needs to be disrupted—is the one of "it's just about spending more money on what we're already doing." In fact, it's the existing approaches that are holding the problem in place.

You don't find hostile camps so much as folks whose view of homelessness has gone unchallenged for a long time. Across the political spectrum, what's shared is a lack of accountability for solving the problem.

The work of Built for Zero right now involves eighty-nine communities across the country. They are almost evenly split between red and blue communities, and all participation is voluntary. Do you see differences in uptake?

We see that in communities where there aren't ideological battles, the work of reducing homelessness goes faster.

Can you give an example of that?

Well, New York is one example of a place caught in ideological battles. In New York, $3.2 billion is spent annually on an emergency shelter system, much of it

"Homelessness is a dynamic problem. It's not a static problem. People transition in and out of it. But for years, the assumption has been different."

Rosanne Haggerty

privatized and operated by not-for-profits and private landlords and hotel operators. Despite this massive spending, homelessness has continued to rise. Yet the city continues to do more of what is not working rather than honestly assess the policies that perpetuate this broken system. Homelessness has become an industry in New York City, and political leaders have shied away from accountability for reducing homelessness or even challenging the assumptions, policies, and behaviors that preserve the status quo.

What is an example of a community where homelessness is brought down really well, without ideological battles?

Take the Gulf Coast of Mississippi, a six-county region with a population of about 600,000. They have ended veteran homelessness; they are very close to ending chronic homelessness. They may well be the first community in the country to just end homelessness altogether. This is a place with very few resources coming from the state government, but the local team is strong and very well led. Now, housing costs are lower there, and of course the rates of homelessness in Gulf Coast are very different from a place like New York City. But it is the willingness of Gulf Coast leaders to collaborate to achieve population-level reductions in homelessness, to use data, to share a common view of the problem, to assess what's working, and to make changes as a result that is remarkable. It's been very impressive to see.

Jacksonville, Florida, is another community—vast in terms of their geography. They have made profound progress toward ending veteran homelessness, again without lots of new state or local resources.

Which underlines your earlier point—it's less about how much money we spend, and more about how we work together. By the way: How literal do we need to take the goal of ending homelessness?

What a community team signs up for when they join Built for Zero is getting to a racially equitable and sustainable end to homelessness—with our support and the support of other participating communities. And let me share the definition of "end" in this context: It means the community is staying ahead of homelessness and has a very robust, almost public health–quality data monitoring system, is capable of quickly flagging new cases of homelessness, and then swiftly and effectively resolving them.

That's the goal we are working toward. This definition of "functional zero," another concept borrowed from public health, describes this state of staying ahead of the problem. We have learned from disease eradication efforts that success is not a one-time achievement but requires a local system that is continuously preventing and quickly resolving new incidents of homelessness.

It's interesting to see how you are working both hyperlocal—down to the specificities of cities and counties, each with their own experiences and approaches—but at the same time nationally, with a view on data, patterns, and systemic intervention.

Well, I think what we are learning is that a) it's possible to solve complex problems at scale while being place-based, and b) the need for community actors to work toward shared, measurable aims to overcome the typical fragmentation of efforts. Otherwise, the work being done in each community at a given time remains specific to each community's situation.

It's a process not only for ending homelessness but for organizing collective action...

...that can be applied to other fields?

The methodology has relevance for many other questions—we know this in part because we have borrowed and recruited experts from other fields: public health, manufacturing, even software design, architecture—fields where people are trained to think in systems and improve how teams work, how to practice accountability for results, how to use data for learning, not judgment, how to make progress through small tests of change and see "failure" as part of the learning process.

Have academics played a role?

So far, not directly, no. But we've worked and exchanged ideas with other "zero" initiatives—zero suicides in the health care system, zero avoidable medical errors, zero traffic accidents. We find we all have in common a focus on population-level approaches and the rigorous use of data and have all learned a lot from great public health victories. Organizing a whole community of data-driven changemakers collaborating towards the same goal is what distinguishes our approaches.

Rosanne Haggerty spoke with Konstanze Frischen and Michael Zakaras.

Rosanne Haggerty is the founder of Community Solutions. Community Solutions is a nonprofit working to create a lasting end to homelessness that leaves no one behind. It leads Built for Zero, a national initiative of more than eighty cities and counties committed to measurably and equitably ending homelessness. Using a data-driven methodology, these communities have changed how local homeless response systems work and the impact they can achieve. To date, fourteen communities have achieved "functional zero" homelessness for one or more populations. Forty-seven communities have achieved a measurable reduction, and eighty-two communities now have real-time data on all those experiencing homelessness, an essential part of an effective system that is making homelessness rare overall and brief when it occurs.

Community Solutions also supports national initiatives in Great Britain, Denmark, Australia, and Canada modeled on Built for Zero.

In 2021, the organization was awarded the MacArthur Foundation's prestigious 100&Change award, which funds a single $100 million proposal that promises real and measurable progress in solving a critical problem of our time.

Democracy Reborn

Eric Liu

Democracies are sustained not just by laws and elections, argues Eric Liu, but by a culture of powerful, responsible citizenship. With democracy under threat in the United States and around the world, how do we create the spaces and habits for rekindling and nurturing that culture at the local level? A conversation about faith, responsibility, power, and America as an ongoing argument.

Eric, you speak of democracy in the United States as a "creed," which we tend to associate with religious faith. Is democracy a religion?

Well, I would say that democracy works only if enough of us believe democracy works. The process of self-government involves policy and legal structure and institutions, but what animates it all is civic spirit—a belief that participating in the first place will yield benefits. What we're seeing in the United States right now and around the world is that democracy is not inevitable. It is not self-perpetuating. The belief in democracy requires constant nurturing and cultivation. And that belief has to emerge from the inside out: Showing up in this diverse community is something that I should want to do because it benefits me and those around me.

In our country's case, we are bound together by very little besides, number one, mass consumer capitalism, and number two, our underlying civic creed. We cannot simply be the United States of Subway, McDonald's, and KFC. We have to be the United States of America in a way that makes us take seriously the idea of liberty and justice for all, equal protection of the laws, we the people. Some may be cynical or think that these words are clichés. But our democracy is healthy to the extent that people left and right, young and old, actually take them seriously. And that doesn't mean blind faith! When I say "belief" I mean a belief that is tested by trial, by constant questioning and even upheaval, by pushing ourselves and our institutions to live up to the principles and promises of our stated high ideals.

Are believing in democracy and believing in the United States synonymous?

Democracy as it plays out in any society—whether it's Germany or South Korea or its final flickers right now in Hong Kong—is part of a larger cultural story and unique history. The United States is a nation born of a creed, but with its birth came a foundational hypocrisy that undermined that very creed. We are left with this complicated legacy of deciding over and over again in every generation: Is democracy, is our nation, worth keeping, or should we throw these ideas aside? Over and over again—for all our frustrations and bitterness and anger about the gap—we decide to keep the creed.

As we ask that question over and over again, are we losing faith?

People in all societies have dreams. But when I say "I have a dream" in the American context, I am making a reference not only to Martin Luther King, I'm making a reference to an ongoing struggle about race and American identity, and the way in which Americanness has to transcend whiteness in order to achieve its full promise. So in the United States to believe in democracy is not only to believe in the idea of America, but to face our history and face ourselves in full. The debates that are happening right now about critical race theory and the teaching of American history are just the latest in a regular spasm that we have as a country as we ask the question: "Who is 'us'?"

Does that worry you?

Well, whether at the level of individual psychology or collective sociology, in times of transition you get both identity crisis and crisis of faith. We are going through two simultaneous tectonic shifts right now in the United States. One is this demographic shift, in which it is now within sight that we will be a majority people of color nation, and where we are contesting the meaning of Americanness and the dominance of whiteness. The second tectonic shift is a multi-decade concentration of wealth and power and economic clout in the United States that has given us a raw politics of a great pushback, on both the left and the right, against an entrenched small number of elites. People believe the game is rigged. And what many thought was the basis of their identity and dignity and relative status is shifting.

I believe firmly that this crisis is an opening—a birthing. It is an opportunity. And I try to put it in the affirmative: What we're doing in the United States right now is hard, because it's hard. We're trying to be the planet's first successful mass multi-racial, multi-faith, multi-cultural democratic republic. No other society has hit all those marks before. To me that is exciting.

And you have a unique vantage point for how this plays out at the local level among ordinary citizens.

Yes. Our flagship program, Civic Saturdays, emerged in late 2016 out of that particular moment of identity crisis in the United States. Civic Saturdays are a civic analogue to a faith gathering. We gather friends and strangers together to nurture a spirit of shared purpose—to connect around the values and practices of being an active citizen. We've been training people, civic catalysts from communities that range from a town of five hundred to cities of many millions, to lead these gatherings.

What lessons do you draw from what you are seeing?

These gatherings are growing and spreading all across the country, and one of the reasons is that they are rooted in place. Despite a very similar structure and spirit, Civic Saturdays play out differently wherever they happen because they represent the incredible diversity of place and local identity in the United States. And that, to me, shows part of the way out of our democracy crisis. At the national level, in our media and politics, we are often presented with false choices and abstractions that start to evaporate when you get back to the level of Wichita, Kansas, or Athens, Tennessee, or San Diego, California, or Brownsville, Minnesota.

We create a space for people to reckon with our history, to reckon with our creed, but in a much more relational way than national politics allows. And in a more forgiving way. At the local level still, people are able, willing, and in a certain sense obligated to maintain bonds of trust. It's not as easy to just completely flame and torch someone you disagree with who's an actual neighbor and might actually bump into you on Main Street over and over again, as compared to doing it anonymously on social media.

At the local level, people can show up as their full, complex, contradictory selves and not get slotted into the binaries of contemporary politics. They might disagree on this president or this policy or this approach to cultural politics. Yet they still have to solve something in their town. Civic Saturdays are a great window into, and I hope an accelerator of, the sense of bottom-up responsibility-taking that in the end is going to be the only thing that actually helps us achieve America.

Does it require loving America to participate? Or is it sufficient to love democracy, or to love your town?

I personally feel very comfortable speaking about a love of country and a love of America; others may speak more about a love of Winona or a love of Nashville.

But again when I speak about love of America, that is not a blind love. Patriotism, true patriotism, is not jingoism. It is not rah-rah-we're-number-one-ism. Instead, I think of what the great German immigrant Carl Schurz said. Over 150 years ago he fled failed attempts to democratize Germany, came to the U.S., became a general in the Union Army, and later a United States senator from Missouri. Just like today, he was living during a time of rising nativism and slogans like "My country, right or wrong." But he pushed back and offered a rebuttal to that: "My country—when right, to be kept right; when wrong, to be set right."

That captures the dualism of responsibility. When things are going well, you have to ask how we can sustain what's going well. But when things are manifestly going wrong, whether it's on racial injustice or the climate crisis or economic inequality, then you have this doubled obligation to say, "What can I be doing to mobilize others and activate others to fix this, to remedy it, and to actually close that gap?" This is the kind of patriotism I feel comfortable preaching about and that I hope we all get comfortable practicing. Where we invite each other to question our faith, express doubt, vocalize cynicism. It will play out differently in different places, but underpinned by a common spirit.

Of course the world today, compared to the world of Carl Schurz, is very different. Today, people are fed an unending stream of information and misinformation almost designed to keep us angry at each other, keep us in our tribes. Does it sometimes feel like you're swimming against a tidal wave?

So, two things. Number one, let me acknowledge in the first place what Citizen University is doing here—and I would say what every Ashoka Fellow in the United States is doing—is on some level countercultural. The dominant culture of the United States right now is atomistic, hyper-individualistic, super-materialistic; it is memoryless, it is all about now. It is all about immediate gratification, right? And that's largely because it's a market culture, but it's also because, again, we're a mass entertainment culture.

At Citizen University we embrace that this is countercultural, that we're pushing a way of living that is about understanding where you are in a stream of history and not just the eternal now, that civic duty is about responsibilities and not just rights.

Yes.

And the second thing: We Americans continuously have a choice. It is true that our structures, and our economy, and our media ecosystem, tip the scales in that choice-making and make it easier to get the satisfaction of an angry Twitter feed. But we still retain choice. Our message at Citizen University is that a culture of civic responsibility begins with taking responsibility for yourself. Self-government begins with "govern thyself." How do you govern yourself in what you consume? No one's force-feeding me to go on Twitter all the time. Or to only follow people I agree with. We do have a measure of agency that we must not surrender. And it's only if we reclaim that agency and that power that we'll have anything like a shot at changing our culture in the United States.

That's a helpful reminder. On the historical point again for a minute, as you've said the U.S. has had many phases of sort of hyper-nationalism and tribalism. In January 2021, we witnessed an insurrection on the Capitol. It seems like the left is serious about protecting American democracy whereas for many on the right, the allegiance is to party and person over country. Is what we are seeing today different in scope and scale, and more dangerous than what we've seen in the past?

It is more dangerous. And for those of us who work on trying to remake our democracy in the United States, it requires not getting caught in the box of bipartisanship. Or let me put it this way: The best formulation of this comes from Alexis de Tocqueville, who spoke of people being not necessarily partisans for Republicans or Democrats, but partisans for *democracy.* I'm a partisan for democracy. And if you're a partisan for democracy, then you have to let the chips fall where they will fall, and you have to be willing to name where they have fallen.

In my own voting life, yes, I vote Democratic, but it is not as a Democrat, it is as a partisan for small-d democracy that I will point out that the national Republican Party has been co-opted, by not only the cult figure of a former president, but by an authoritarian approach to politics, that is undermining small-d democracy itself. And that is corrosive and dangerous. If one of our two major political parties is overrun by anti-democratic intentions, then

"We're trying to be the planet's first successful mass multi-racial, multi-faith, multi-cultural democratic republic. No other society has hit all those marks before. To me that is exciting."

"Knowing your own mind is the only antidote, at the end of the day, to all the disinformation, misinformation, and the mechanization of lies that is poisoning the body politic. We are the immune system."

Eric Liu

the highest order is not bipartisanship, the highest order is the defense of democracy.

We're with you.

Where I differ from what you said is, it's not just the left that wants to defend democracy; there are people across the full ideological spectrum who want to contain the people who are insurrectionists and who feed that cult of personality and grievance and authoritarianism. In that effort, I want to align with partisans of democracy who are conservative, partisans of democracy who are libertarian, partisans of democracy who are elected Republican officials, partisans of democracy who disagree with me on every policy issue down the line, but who at the end of the day want to contain that illiberal authoritarian force that's arising on the right—and by the way, on the left as well.

In terms of the politicians that you would say are standing for democracy, do you think they are doing a good job right now? And if not, what could they do better?

I recently coauthored a report via the American Academy of Arts and Sciences—an institution born before the United States was fully born, while we were fighting the Revolutionary War—that was called "Our Common Purpose." It was informed by over fifty listening sessions in communities of all kinds with constituencies of all kinds around the United States. One set of recommendations is about fostering a new culture of civic responsibility-taking. But then there are other recommendations that are about the structural changes that have to happen, like changing how we do redistricting. National-level changes and local-level changes. We have to have a vast flotilla—a diverse ragtag band of civic efforts—to do this.

I don't put it on politicians only. Do I wish there were more political leaders who could defy some of these trends and put country over party? Yes. But I also recognize that most of the time, most of what we call elected leaders are not leaders. They are exquisitely attuned followers. They will listen for demand signals, and they will follow where they think the heat is. And so it's up to us—we the people—to create more noise as partisans for democracy and be able to reward and incent candidates and office—holders to start moving in the direction that we're talking about here.

But these days even the singing of our national anthem at sporting events has become politicized. So where are the cultural elements that create that kind of unity and cohesion?

This may sound paradoxical, but I think one of the most important aspects of what it means to be an American is arguing over what it means to be an American. I'm not one who wants to find a magical consensus. I think there's actually great potential and beauty in constant disputation over the meaning of our nation, our nation's identity, our nation's history, and our nation's symbols.

America, when you understand it properly, is an argument. America is an argument between a Hamiltonian view of strong central government and a Jeffersonian view of limited government and local control. America is an argument between an ideal of colorblindness and an imperative for color consciousness. It is an argument between the pluribus part of our national motto and the unum part of our national motto. We're not meant to have consensus or unanimity around any of those polarities; rather we're meant to be continually in tension.

The commitment we have to make, which is more easily done at the local level than via national politics, is to humanize the people I'm arguing with and not turn them into demonized, disposable entities. And we also have to commit to the process itself: of winning some and losing some, of figuring it out together. You mention the national anthem. I'm a huge baseball fan, and I grew up a Yankees fan. Which means I was raised to tribally hate the Red Sox, right? And yet I share with them an interest in the underlying health of the game itself. When baseball itself becomes corrupted, rigged, broken by steroids or gambling, that happens to the detriment of us all, and we have a common interest in sustaining the game itself.

That's a great analogy. But does it work—all of us arm in arm, committed to the integrity of the game—in a post-truth era? When we are arguing about what we are seeing in front of our very eyes being true or not?

I remain relatively hopeful on this count, for two reasons. One is historically we've had plenty of times in American history when everyone had their own truth. It's only been a feature of the post-war era that we even have an expectation that media should be objective. So we have contended with this ontological contest of defining reality, even if the speed and ubiquity of it today is greater. The second reason goes back to this idea of individual responsibility. Every one of us has an obligation to know our own minds. What do we actually believe and why? Do I believe this just because my neighbors believe this? Do I believe this because it's what my parents told me? Have I actually spent even a minute thinking about my theory of where prosperity comes from and why I'm either for or against higher taxation of the wealthy? Have I interrogated my own heart about why I have this reflex about Black Lives Matter? Knowing your own mind is the only antidote, at the end of the day, to all the disinformation, misinformation, and the mechanization of lies that is poisoning the body politic. We are the immune system.

Eric, you've written: "Power is a gift. Every day we give it away." What do you mean by that?

A lot of the work we do at Citizen University is about simply teaching power: understanding what it is, how it works, who has it, and why. When you begin to look at power not as a dirty thing over there that I don't want to get involved in, but actually as something that is in all of our lives all of the time, you begin to realize how even the most seemingly powerless of us has power. You have voice, you have a capacity to organize and mobilize other people. You have a way to influence the social norms of those around you. As few dollars as you might have, you have the ability to activate other people to spend or withhold their dollars.

Once you take inventory of your civic and social capital, you realize how often you are wasting it and giving it away thoughtlessly. That's probably most manifest in the way that people don't vote, because as I've often said, there is no such thing as not voting. Not voting is voting. Not voting is actively choosing to give your power over to someone else whose interests will often be inimical to your own. But what is true of voting literally is true of so many other things figuratively. We are giving our power away by not engaging, not participating, not activating, not knowing our own minds or even our own hearts.

But you are also forced to decide with your power: Shall I hoard it or shall I circulate it? We live in a time of deep and deepening inequality, where all the pressures and the instincts are toward hoarding—a scarcity mindset. And the pandemic has taught us this rather vividly, hasn't it? We fill our pantries with toilet paper. But what this time demands of us, actually, is to circulate our power, circulate our knowledge, and our social capital. Because what the pandemic also taught us, painfully, is that at the end of the day there's no such thing as someone else's problem. Everyone's problem is contagious. There is no wall high enough to guard you against not only a virus, but to guard you against ultimately the virus of rampant inequality and concentration of wealth.

We're all better off when we're all better off. The magic comes when you really start to experience those words at the local level—when you begin to see people in a different light and shed that reflex toward hoarding and zero-sum approaches to money, race, gender. When you recognize that we're all in this together.

Eric Liu spoke with Konstanze Frischen and Michael Zakaras.

Eric Liu is the co-founder of Citizen University. Citizen University is building a culture of powerful, responsible citizenship across the country, envisioning a civic revival across the nation where Americans are steeped in a sense of civic character, educated in the tools of civic power, and are problem-solving contributors in a self-governing community.

Citizen University spreads the belief that a strong democracy depends on strong citizens—having the power to make change in civic life and the responsibility to try. The organization designs gatherings, rituals, and workshops that focus on civic power and civic character as the building blocks of powerful citizenship. It then trains and activates civic catalysts nationwide to bring the beliefs and practices of powerful, responsible citizenship to their communities.

Contributors

Cahn, Albert Fox

Albert Fox Cahn is the Surveillance Technology Oversight Project's (S.T.O.P.'s) founder and executive director, and an Ashoka social entrepreneur. He is also a fellow at Yale Law School's Information Society Project, NYU School of Law's Engelberg Center on Innovation Law & Policy, and the Day One Project. As a lawyer, technologist, writer, and interfaith activist, Mr. Cahn began S.T.O.P. in the belief that emerging surveillance technologies pose an unprecedented threat to civil rights and the promise of a free society.

Mr. Cahn is a frequent commentator on civil rights, privacy, and technology matters. He is a contributor to the *New York Times*, *the Boston Globe*, *the Guardian*, *WIRED*, *Slate*, *NBC Think*, *Newsweek*, and dozens of other publications. He has lectured at Harvard Law School, New York University School of Law, Columbia University, and Dartmouth College. Mr. Cahn previously served as an associate at Weil, Gotshal & Manges LLP, where he advised Fortune 50 companies on technology policy, antitrust law, and consumer privacy.

In addition to his work at S.T.O.P., Mr. Cahn serves on the New York Immigration Coalition's Immigrant Leaders Council and the New York Immigrant Freedom Fund's Advisory Council, and is an editorial board member for the Anthem Ethics of Personal Data Collection. Mr. Cahn received his J.D., cum laude, from Harvard Law School (where he was an editor of the Harvard Law & Policy Review) and his B.A. in politics and philosophy from Brandeis University.

Cancel, Sixto

Sixto Cancel grew up in, and aged out of, the child welfare system. His personal lived experience has powered a passion to transform the child welfare system so that all foster youth have conditions that allow them to Heal, Develop, and Thrive. Sixto believes that centering the lived experiences of people whose lives are touched by the system—foster youth, foster parents, caregivers, caseworkers, judges, and funders—allows us to co-design solutions and shift the dynamics that hold problems in place. He is the founder of Think of Us and, alongside his team, is committed to total transformation of child welfare in the United States.

Sixto is an Ashoka Fellow. He was named a 2017 Forbes Top 30 Under 30 Social Entrepreneur and serves on the 2021 Forbes Under 30 Lister Board. Recognized by the White House as a Champion of Change, as a Millennial Maker by BET, and as one of the Top 24 Changemakers in Government Under 24 in the country by the Campaign for a Presidential Youth Council and SparkAction, Sixto has served as CEO of Think of Us since 2017. He has played a key role in the work of extending foster care and permanency for older youth as a Young Fellow at the Jim Casey Youth Opportunities Initiative. He is also an alumnus of Clinton Global Initiative University and FastForward.

Dennison, Brandon

Brandon is Ashley Dennison's husband and father to their boys: Owen and Will. Born and raised in West Virginia, he is founder and CEO of Coalfield Development, which incubates social enterprises designed to diversify Appalachia's coal-based economy and cultivate opportunity for people facing barriers to employment. Dennison graduated from Shepherd University with a B.A. in history. He holds a master of public affairs from Indiana University. In 2017, Brandon was named West Virginian of the Year by *WV Living* magazine. He is an Ashoka Fellow. He is the winner of the JMK Social Innovation Prize and a Draper Richards Kaplan Entrepreneur. In 2019, Brandon was awarded the Heinz Award for Economy and Employment. He recently testified before Congress on how the Coalfield model could be used to combat climate change, and he currently serves as Entrepreneur in Residence at Marshall University. For ten years, he has tried to learn the guitar but still only knows eight or nine songs (importantly, "Country Roads" is one of those).

Being born and raised in West Virginia, Brandon never forgot seeing people his own age desperate for jobs. In 2010, Brandon founded Coalfield Development to respond to poverty in Appalachia through on-the-job training, higher education, and mentorship. The organization's story is featured in a film that premiered at the Tribeca Film Festival: *From the Ashes*.

Dixon, T. Morgan

T. Morgan Dixon is the co-founder and CEO of GirlTrek, the largest health movement for Black women in America. Through national campaigns, community leadership, and health advocacy, GirlTrek mobilizes Black women to be changemakers in their lives and communities. GirlTrek has so far rallied (as of June 2021) more than 1.5 million Black women to walk for their health and the health of their communities. Prior to GirlTrek, Dixon was on the front lines of education reform. She served as director of leadership development for one of the largest charter school networks in the country, Achievement First, and direct-

ed the start-up of six public schools in New York City for St. Hope and the Urban Assembly. She has served as a trustee for boards of the National Outdoor Leadership School, Teach for Haiti, and the Harriet Tubman Underground Railroad Byway, a $50 million tourism and preservation project in Maryland. Dixon is an Ashoka Fellow. As the co-leader of GirlTrek, Dixon has also received fellowships from Teach for America, Echoing Green, and the Aspen Institute. She has been featured in *the New York Times* and on CNN, was named a "health hero" by *Essence* magazine, and has appeared on the cover of Outside magazine's "Icons" edition. She got a standing ovation during her TED Talk in 2017 with over 1 million views and earned a grant from the Audacious Project, the newest iteration of the TED Prize, a selective cohort of global organizations that receive eight-figure investments.

Ezeilo, Angelou

Angelou's love for the environment stretches back to when she was a little girl who had the chance to escape the dense urban streets of Jersey City, New Jersey, to summer in her family's home in upstate New York. After a brief stint of practicing law, it was through her work as a legal specialist for the New Jersey State Agriculture and Development Committee that Angelou embarked upon a career as an environmentalist. She further honed her skills as a project manager for the Trust for Public Land, where she acquired land for preservation and worked on the New York–New Jersey Highlands Program, Parks for People–Newark, the New York–New Jersey Harbor Program, the Atlanta Beltline, and the 20 County Regional Greenspace Initiative in Georgia. While at the Trust for Public Land, Angelou realized the disconnect between the land that was being preserved and the education and participation of people. This was the impetus for the Greening Youth Foundation. Angelou is an Ashoka Fellow. She is a graduate of Spelman College, Georgia. She received her juris doctorate in law from the University of Florida College of Law. Angelou is a member of the

National Center for Civil and Human Rights' Women's Solidarity Society and Georgia Audubon boards, an advisory board member for Outdoor Afro, MillionMile Greenway, Keeping It Wild, and Rachel's Network, and most recently the author of *Engage, Connect, Protect: Empowering Diverse Youth as Environmental Leaders.*

Angelou is a lover of cultural dance, hiking and birds, and good avocado toast! As recent empty nesters, Angelou and her husband of twenty-five years split their time between Atlanta, Georgia, and Lagos, Nigeria.

Haggerty, Rosanne

Rosanne Haggerty is the president and CEO of Community Solutions. She is an internationally recognized leader in developing innovative strategies to end homelessness and strengthen communities. Community Solutions assists communities throughout the U.S. and internationally in solving the complex housing problems facing their most vulnerable residents. Their large-scale change initiatives include the 100,000 Homes and Built for Zero campaigns to end homelessness, and neighborhood partnerships that bring together local residents and institutions to change the conditions that produce homelessness. Earlier, she founded Common Ground Community, a pioneer in the design and development of supportive housing and research-based practices that end homelessness. Ms. Haggerty is an Ashoka Fellow. She was a Japan Society Public Policy Fellow and is a MacArthur Foundation Fellow, Schwab Foundation Social Entrepreneur, Hunt Alternative Fund Prime Mover, and the recipient of honors including the Jane Jacobs Medal for New Ideas and Activism from the Rockefeller Foundation, Cooper Hewitt/Smithsonian Design Museum's National Design Award, and Independent Sector's John W. Gardner Leadership Award. She is a graduate of Amherst College and Columbia University's Graduate School of Architecture, Planning and Preservation.

Hemminger, Sarah

Sarah Hemminger is a social entrepreneur, scientist, and ice dancer who co-founded Thread, a nonprofit that harnesses the power of relationships to support exceptional young people facing significant opportunity and achievement gaps.

Sarah has overseen the development, expansion, and replication of an innovative, paradigm-shifting model that has led to exemplary outcomes for young people and a deeply knitted community of thousands of diverse Baltimoreans. This work fuels her belief that building strong relationships across lines of difference can end social isolation and weave a more equitable social fabric that improves educational, economic, and health outcomes.

Sarah is an Ashoka Fellow. She has been awarded fellowships from Echoing Green, Open Society Institute, and the Albert Schweitzer Fellows Program. Her work has been covered by *the New York Times, Forbes,* and *the Chronicle of Philanthropy.* She has been a featured speaker at the Aspen Ideas Festival, the White House, the Smithsonian Symposium on American Philanthropy, TEDxWashington Square, TEDxBaltimore, and Emerson Collective's Demo Day.

Sarah received her undergraduate degree and Ph.D. in biomedical engineering from the Johns Hopkins University. Her work on the role of the cerebellum and the primary motor cortex on the time scales of consolidation of motor memory was published in the *Journal of Neuroscience, Journal of Neurophysiology,* and *Cerebral Cortex.* She received the prestigious Siebel Scholars award for outstanding work in the field of technology and engineering.

Sarah is an adjunct assistant professor at Johns Hopkins and serves as the board chair of Thrive, a for-profit technology company.

Jackson, William

William Jackson is the founder and chief dreamer of Village of Wisdom, an organization that is mobilizing a nationwide movement of families to celebrate and protect their children's Black genius. At age twenty-four, Will became the highest performing science teacher in his district but yearned to expand his impact. Consequently, he decided to pursue and complete a Ph.D. in education at the University of North Carolina, and later, to start Village of Wisdom. He leads a team of colleagues whose daily mission is to translate the wisdom of Black parents into strategies that will create more culturally affirming learning environments for Black learners. Will is an Ashoka Fellow and has also been awarded Echoing Green, Camelback Ventures, and Education Pioneer fellowships.

Jayadev, Raj

Raj Jayadev is co-founder of Silicon Valley De-Bug, a storytelling, community organizing, and advocacy nonprofit based in San Jose, California. The organization has become a leading voice in community activism, using Raj's multimedia platforms, advocacy, and community organizing to spread social change messages and engage in community building. As an outgrowth of his organizing and advocacy work, Raj has become a nationally recognized pioneer in criminal defense reform. He is an Ashoka Fellow. He is also a 2010 Soros Justice Fellow, a 2015 Leading Edge Fellow, a 2017 Stanford Entrepreneur in Residence, and a 2018 MacArthur Fellow. His work has been featured in the *New York Times*, *Time*, NPR, PBS, *the Atlantic*, and various other news outlets. Raj holds a B.A. in political science from the University of California, Los Angeles.

Lampkin, Tim

Tim Lampkin is the founder and CEO of Higher Purpose Co., a 501c3 economic justice nonprofit building community wealth with Black residents across Mississippi by supporting the ownership of financial, cultural, and political power. In 2021, Ashoka recognized Lampkin as its first Mississippi-based social entrepreneur. *The Mississippi Business*

Journal selected Lampkin as one of the 2019 Top Entrepreneurs in the state. He is a former Common Future Fellow and Movement Voices Fellow. Tim has over a decade of community development and entrepreneurship experience. He previously managed the Racial Equity Program for the Mississippi Humanities Council, which won the national 2018 Schwartz Prize. Lampkin also worked for Southern Bancorp Community Partners to implement community initiatives. He assisted rural entrepreneurs at Delta State University in five rural counties. He continues to produce narrative change documentaries highlighting relevant Mississippi topics.

Lampkin serves on the board of the Cooperative Food Empowerment Directive and previously served a three-year term on the Federal Reserve Bank of St. Louis Community Development Advisory Council. He was recently appointed to the Consumer Financial Protection Bureau's Consumer Advisory Board. He is a proud HBCU graduate of Mississippi Valley State University and is currently finishing a doctor of education degree at the University of Arkansas.

Lingane, Alison

Alison Lingane has dedicated her career to enabling business to be a force for good. She is the co-founder of Project Equity, a national leader in the movement to harness employee ownership to maintain thriving local business communities, create quality jobs, and address income and wealth inequality. Her passion for creating quality jobs and an economy that works for everyone was fueled in her early career by her role designing and leading micro-enterprise programs for urban youth. While getting her MBA, she co-founded what is now the Global Social Venture Competition, the largest international business plan competition for double or triple bottom line businesses. Prior to launching Project Equity, Alison spent fifteen years in senior leadership roles in mission-driven companies that are designed to create human impact at scale.

She now brings those scaling lessons back full circle to her work at Project Equity, turning businesses into community change agents through employee ownership.

A serial social entrepreneur, in 2006 Alison co-founded a thriving PreK-to-eighth-grade dual immersion school (Escuela Bilingüe Internacional) in Oakland, California, that now serves over 360 students. Alison has a B.A. from Harvard University and an M.B.A. from the Haas School of Business at the University of California, Berkeley. She is an Ashoka Fellow and has been selected as an Echoing Green Fellow and an Aspen Institute Job Quality Fellow.

Liu, Eric

Eric Liu is the co-founder and CEO of Citizen University. He also directs the Aspen Institute's Citizenship and American Identity Program. He is the author of eight books, including *The Accidental Asian: Notes of a Native Speaker; The Gardens of Democracy: A New American Story of Citizenship, the Economy, and the Role of Government* (co-authored with Nick Hanauer); *You're More Powerful Than You Think: A Citizen's Guide to Making Change Happen*; and *Become America: Civic Sermons on Love, Responsibility, and Democracy*. Eric served as a White House speechwriter for President Bill Clinton and later as White House deputy domestic policy advisor. He was appointed by President Barack Obama to the board of the Corporation for National and Community Service and has served on the Washington State Board of Education and the Seattle Public Library board of trustees. He is an Ashoka Fellow and a member of the American Academy of Arts and Sciences. Eric lives in Seattle with his family.

Livingston, Denisa

Denisa Livingston(Diné), is an unapologetic food justice organizer, committed to addressing food apartheid and nutritional trauma in Indigenous communities. She is an Ashoka Fellow, a Slow Food Interna-

tional Indigenous Councilor of the Global North, and an appointed member of the Champions Network of the United Nations' Food Systems Summit. Denisa has been a legislative speaker and community health advocate for the Diné Community Advocacy Alliance, which has been globally recognized for the successful passage of several laws, the first of their kind: Elimination of Tax on Healthy Foods with an emphasis on Indigenous foods, the Healthy Diné Nation Act of 2014, or Unhealthy Foods Tax, and a tax revenue allocation for community wellness projects for all 110 Navajo chapters. She has been addressing and raising awareness of the widening disparities and injustices caused by the COVID-19 pandemic in Indigenous communities.

Denisa holds a master of public health degree from the University of Nevada, Las Vegas. She is a member of the advisory board of the Slow Food Indigenous Peoples international network—Indigenous Terra Madre, a member of the Slow Food Turtle Island Association steering committee, a member of a national Sugar Action Group, a former advisory member of the groundbreaking initiative Reclaiming Native Truth: A Project to Dispel America's Myths and Misconceptions, and she is currently on the Seeds of Native Health Research Conference committee and a member of the Slow Food USA Equity, Inclusion, and Justice Working Group. She is one of the contributors to the newly published anthology *Food Sovereignty in the United States: Restoring Cultural Knowledge, Protecting Environments, and Regaining Health*. The work and efforts of Denisa focus on servant leadership, gastronomy, creating new roles for society, and bridging community members to purpose and innovation.

Lubell, David

David Lubell is a leader in a global movement supporting the proliferation of more welcoming and inclusive communities. In 2009, David founded and became the executive director of

Welcoming America. Welcoming America has been recognized worldwide for its innovative approach to immigrant and refugee inclusion, including by the United Nations Alliance of Civilizations and the Obama White House. In 2018, David shifted his full-time focus to the organization's international efforts as the founding director of the Welcoming International Initiative. He leads this initiative from Berlin, Germany. Welcoming International supports institutions across the world building bottom-up movements for immigrant and refugee inclusion in their countries. The initiative is now supporting rapidly expanding efforts in Australia, Canada, Germany, Mexico, New Zealand, Spain, and the U.K.

David is also the founder and former executive director of the Tennessee Immigrant and Refugee Rights Coalition, which has grown into a model for immigrant rights organizing throughout the U.S.A Wesleyan University graduate, he received a master's degree in public administration from the Harvard Kennedy School. David is an Ashoka Fellow. He is also a recipient of several other fellowships, including those from Draper Richards Kaplan Foundation and Harvard. He is also a World Economic Forum Young Global Leader and was named to the 2016 Chronicle of Philanthropy's 40 Under 40 list. In 2017, David was awarded the Charles Bronfman Prize, which recognizes one young humanitarian annually whose work is inspired by their Jewish values and is of universal benefit to all people.

Miller, Mauricio Lim

Mauricio Lim Miller is a Mexican American social entrepreneur, public speaker, and author. He is the son of a hardworking, strong, and creative single mother who immigrated to the U.S. from Mexico. Mauricio saw that his mother, a talented dressmaker who worked hard to "make it" in America, wanted more access and opportunity for him and his sister. He was certain there was a better way to invest in people's initiative than what his mother had experienced. He also knew firsthand the

harmful stereotypes and belief systems that perpetuated biased practices and policies, undermining the pride of those being "helped" and their chances for success.

He was affiliated with Asian Neighborhood Design (1978–2000) before founding the Family Independence Initiative in Oakland, California, in 2001, and the Community Independence Initiative in 2019. Miller is a leader in the development of services and systems designed to break the cycle of economic dependency for low-income families across the United States. He received a number of recognitions and awards for his work, including a "Genius Grant" from the John D. and Catherine T. MacArthur Foundation in 2012. He has been an Ashoka Fellow since 2011. Miller received B.S. and M.A. degrees from the University of California, Berkeley. In 2019–2020, Miller was the James Wei Visiting Professor in Entrepreneurship in the Keller Center for Innovation in Engineering Education at Princeton University.

Sered, Danielle

Danielle Sered envisioned, launched, and directs Common Justice. She leads the project's efforts locally and nationally to develop and advance practical and groundbreaking solutions to violence that advance racial equity, meet the needs of those harmed, and do not rely on incarceration. Before planning the launch of Common Justice, Danielle served as the deputy director of the Vera Institute of Justice's Adolescent Reentry Initiative, a program for young men returning from incarceration on Rikers Island, and worked at the Center for Court Innovation's Harlem Community Justice Center. Danielle is an Ashoka Fellow and a Stoneleigh Fellow. She received her B.A. from Emory University and her master's degrees from New York University and Oxford University, where she studied as a Rhodes Scholar. She has been featured widely in the public conversation about mass incarceration and violence, including the Aspen Ideas Festival, the *Atlantic* magazine's Summit on

Race and Justice in America, in *the New York Times*, the *Washington Post*, USA Today, *Democracy Now!*, NPR, and *On Second Thought with Trevor Noah*. Danielle is the author of *The Other Side of Harm: Addressing Disparities in Our Responses to Violence*, of *Accounting for Violence: How to Increase Safety and Break Our Failed Reliance on Mass Incarceration*, and the award-winning book *Until We Reckon: Violence, Mass Incarceration, and a Road to Repair*.

Shorters, Trabian

Trabian Shorters is a *New York Times* best-selling author, social entrepreneur, and the leading authority of an award-winning cognitive framework called Asset-Framing®. His pioneering work in Asset-Framing® earned Shorters recognition as one of the world's leading social entrepreneurs. He is an Ashoka Fellow, a New Pluralist Field Builder, and a member of the Aspen Global Leadership Network. His Asset-Framing® clients include senior executives of the most influential foundations and social impact and public interest communications firms in the U.S.

Shorters's organization, BMe Community, is an award-winning community of Black leaders, builders, and their allies who work to expand freedoms to Live Own Vote and Excel in America.

Shorters is a retired tech entrepreneur, former vice president of the John S. and James L. Knight Foundation, and doting father to two adult sons and two brilliant Black twin girl toddlers who are growing up in the better world that we are making together for them.

Smith, Bren

Bren Smith, GreenWave's co-founder and co–executive director, and owner of Thimble Island Ocean Farm, pioneered the development of regenerative ocean farming. A lifelong commercial fisherman, he was named one of Rolling Stone magazine's "25 People Shaping the Future" and featured in Time magazine's "Best Inventions of 2017." Bren is an Ashoka Fellow. He is the winner of the Buckminster Fuller Challenge and has been profiled by 60 Minutes, CNN, The New Yorker, the Wall Street Journal, National Geographic, and elsewhere. He is an Echoing Green Climate Fellow and James Beard Award–winning author of *Eat Like a Fish: My Adventures Farming the Ocean to Fight Climate Change*.

Soltis, Laura Emiko

A human rights educator originally from rural Minnesota, Emiko was raised in a biracial household as the child of a Japanese pianist and a road construction worker, and developed passions for working-class politics, immigrant rights, and classical music in equal measure. Emiko's work experience alongside immigrants in restaurant work, janitorial services, and farm labor inspired her to study interracial labor movements and international human rights. A proud public school kid, Emiko graduated summa cum laude from the University of Georgia and received her Ph.D. from Emory University. She joined Freedom University as a volunteer faculty member in 2013. Following its closure, she reestablished Freedom University in Atlanta in September 2014, introducing a human rights framework to its mission and pedagogy and connecting undocumented youth to Black student movement veterans. She also founded Freedom University's social movement leadership training program and co-founded the Freedom at Emory Initiative, which led to Emory's decision in 2015 to admit and support undocumented students. As an experienced social movement strategist, Emiko works to advance the undocumented student movement by building bridges between undocumented and documented student groups, and advocating for fair admissions policies in higher education across the U.S. As a professor of human rights and an active public scholar, she writes and lectures on issues such as human rights advocacy, immigration and higher education, and workers' rights and economic justice.

Emiko is an Ashoka Fellow and the recipient of the Telemundo Heroe Luchadora Award and the Ford Foundation's Public Voices Fellowship. Her artistic side finds expression as an accomplished photographer, violinist, and a vocalist in the Atlanta Symphony Orchestra Chamber Chorus. Emiko speaks English, Spanish, and Japanese and enjoys dancing bachata, being a good friend, and loving on her three rescue dogs.

Woods, Casey

Casey Woods is the founder and executive director of FORGE. Casey envisions an America with no gun deaths and believes this future depends on meaningful engagement and partnership with America's fifty million gun owners. Under her leadership, FORGE works from within the firearms community to collaboratively create innovative initiatives, campaigns, and tools to prevent the illegal and unsafe use of guns. Prior to founding FORGE, Casey was an award-winning journalist with extensive experience covering crime, law enforcement, and local government. She is an Ashoka Fellow.

Ashoka Team

Clark, Amy

Amy Clark is part of the leadership team of Ashoka U.S., and joins this project as a co-editor. In her two decades with Ashoka, she has written about hundreds of the world's leading social entrepreneurs and their powerful ideas. She loves collaborating with colleagues and partners across Ashoka to create a world where every person can contribute fully and freely, as changemakers. Amy is a graduate of the University of North Carolina at Chapel Hill.

Frischen, Konstanze

Konstanze Frischen is a member of Ashoka's global leadership group. A social anthropologist and writer by background, she is led by curiosity for how people see the world and why. She founded Ashoka in her native Germany in 2003 and co-led Ashoka's emergence and growth in Western Europe, introducing the then radically new concept of social entrepreneurship. She also co-founded the Globalizer, an initiative re-defining what we mean by scale, and has collaborated with social entrepreneurs from across the globe over the years. She is on the advisory board of CASE at Duke University. She was a writer for CNN and a writer/editor for *Frankfurter Allgemeine Zeitung*, as well as a board member for GLS Bank, Germany's leading ethical financial institution, before moving to the U.S. She is a graduate of the London School of Economics, polyglot, and a mom of two plus four.

Zakaras, Michael

Michael Zakaras is the director of Ashoka U.S. He is also co-founder of Ashoka's "All America" initiative which focuses on pushing the boundaries of social entrepreneurship beyond the traditional coastal circles. Michael has previously worked for Ashoka in Ireland and Central Europe, and has participated on selection panels for social entrepreneurs across the globe, from Montreal to Warsaw to Istanbul. He has a particular interest in food and agriculture policy, criminal justice reform, and more democratic economic models, and writes regularly about these issues and more on *Forbes* online. He grew up in Brussels, has worked in the California wine industry, and holds a master's in public policy from the Harvard Kennedy School of Government.

About Ashoka

Ashoka is the world's largest network of social entrepreneurs. The organization pioneered the field of social entrepreneurship forty years ago and has supported to date almost four thousand Ashoka Fellows across the globe with stipends, catalytic connections, strategic advice, and an unmatched peer community that is for life. Drawing insights from its network, Ashoka identifies and open-sources the underlying patterns of transformative change and has introduced and mainstreamed such words as "social entrepreneur" and "changemaker." Ashoka collaborates with Fellows and partners in more than ninety countries to advance a world where everyone can participate and contribute to solving problems for the good of all: an Everyone a Changemaker society.